# STRIKE
## *the*
# ORIGINAL
# MATCH

## *Books by Chuck Swindoll*
### *Available from Zondervan Publishing House*

Come Before Winter
Encourage Me
For Those Who Hurt
Growing Deep in the Christian Life
Growing Deep in the Christian Life Bible Study Guide
Growing Strong in the Seasons of Life
Killing Giants, Pulling Thorns
The Quest for Character
Second Wind
Stress Fractures
Strike the Original Match
The Strong Family
The Strong Family Bible Study Guide

## *Booklets by Chuck Swindoll*
### *Available from Zondervan Publishing House*

Anger
Attitudes
Commitment: The Key to Marriage
Dealing with Defiance
Demonism: How to Win Against the Devil
Destiny
Divorce: When It All Comes Tumbling Down
Eternal Security
Fun Is Contagious
God's Will
Hope: Our Anchor of the Soul
Impossibilities
Integrity: The Mark of Godliness
Leisure: Having Fun Is Serious Business!
The Lonely Whine of the Top Dog
Moral Purity
Peace in Spite of Panic
Prayer
Sensuality: Resisting the Lure of Lust
Singleness: Biblical Advice on Staying Single
Stress: Calm Answers for the Worry Worn
Tongues: An Answer to Charismatic Confusion
When Your Comfort Zone Gets the Squeeze
Woman: A Person of Worth and Dignity

*When Life's Pressures Have Taken the Warmth*
*Out of Your Marriage . . .*

# STRIKE
## *the*
# ORIGINAL MATCH

## CHARLES R. SWINDOLL

ZondervanPublishingHouse
*Grand Rapids, Michigan*

*A Division of* HarperCollins*Publishers*

*STRIKE THE ORIGINAL MATCH*
Copyright © 1980 by Charles R. Swindoll, Inc.
*Strike the Original Match* © by Charles R. Swindoll, Inc.
*Strike the Original Match Couples Guide* © 1980 by Multnomah Press

Requests for information should be addressed to:
Zondervan Publishing House
Grand Rapids, Michigan 49530

Swindoll, Charles R
    Strike the original match / Charles R. Swindoll.
        p.   cm.
    Originally published: Portland, Or. : Multnomah Press, © 1980 as two
works, Strike the original match, and Strike the original match couples guide.
    ISBN 0-310-41351-6
    1. Marriage—Religious aspects—Christianity. 2. Married people—Religious
life. I. Swindoll, Charles R. Strike the original match couples guide. 1993
II. Title.
    BV835.S95   1993
    248.8'44 – dc20                                                          93–26368
                                                                                CIP

Unless otherwise identified, Scripture references in this volume are from the *New American Standard Bible* © The Lockman Foundation 1960, 1962, 1963, 1968, 1971, 1972, 1973, 1975, 1977. Used by permission.

Verses marked NIV are taken from the Holy Bible, New International Version®. NIV®. Copyright © 1973, 1978, 1984 by International Bible Society. Used by permission of Zondervan Publishing House. All rights reserved.

Verses marked *Living Bible* are from *The Living Bible,* copyright 1971 by Tyndale House Publishers, Wheaton, IL. Used by permission.

*Cover design by* Multnomah Graphics
*Interior book design by* Gary Gnidovic
*Cover photos:*
    © The Stock Market/Mugshots, 1987
    © The Stock Market/Michael Keller, 1991

*Printed in the United States of America*

93 94 95 96 97 / ❖ DH / 10 9 8 7 6 5 4 3 2 1

# Contents

Preface  9

Introduction  11

### 1
### Let's Consult the Architect  17

### 2
### Let's Repair the Foundation  33

### 3
### Bricks That Build a Marriage  47

### 4
### Watch Out for Cheap Substitutes!  67

### 5
### Who Says the Honeymoon Must End?  83

### 6
### Termites in Your Troth  101

### 7
### How to Have a Good Fight  117

### 8
### 'Til Debt Do Us Part  135

### 9
### Divorce: When It All Comes Tumbling Down  159

### 10
### Commitment Is the Key  177

### 11
### Don't Just Get Older, Get Better  197

### 12
### What to Do with an Empty Nest  217

### 13
### Conclusion  227

Discussion Guide  233

Indexes  289

# $\mathcal{P}$reface

$\mathcal{I}$ FINISHED THE ORIGINAL manuscript of this book just as we'd finished remodeling our home back in 1980. The paint was finally dry, the dust had been brushed off the furniture, and we were ready to enjoy the results of a lot of hard work.

And now, over ten years later, as we prepare to reissue *Strike the Original Match*, I have pulled out my writing tools in preparation for a little book remodeling. But as I've read through these pages, I've discovered again that certain things don't change. Like the principles of building a good marriage. Whether you're talking about the honeymoon period or the empty nest, or what builds marriages versus what tears them down, or the principles of managing money and the principles of—I say this carefully—managing "a good fight," the Bible speaks the same language to couples yesterday, today, and tomorrow. In all candor, I've never found better examples demonstrating these truths about marriage than the ones I first included in this book.

So we've decided to reissue this volume as I wrote it. Originally. As Cynthia and I look at the thirty-eight years of our original match, we believe that God can use what's between the covers of this book to help your marriage stay strong, healthy, and full of life. Always.

*Charles R. Swindoll*
Fullerton, California

• • •

# Introduction

WHILE I WRITE these words, strange voices and unusual sounds echo through our house. A layer of drywall dust has settled on most every piece of furniture. The carpet is ripped up and rolled back in two rooms, exposing a cold, bare concrete slab and ugly foam rubber padding. Naked wires dangle where light fixtures once burned brightly, and the downstairs shower is out of commission—and will be until the tile work is finished. The doorbell doesn't work nor does the patio light out back. For almost a week I've seriously considered hanging a sign out front:

DISASTER AREA—ENTER AT YOUR OWN RISK.

Our kids have begun to request maps to help them find their rooms. Not even the dog is sure where she sleeps anymore. Nor am I!

• • •

You guessed it. We're remodeling. Our house is getting an extensive face-lift. In fact, it's more like radical surgery. If you've gone through the process, you don't need any further explanation. If you haven't, you wouldn't believe it if I told you.

There are four things nobody can deny who has endured remodeling:

1. It takes longer than you planned.
2. It costs more than you figured.
3. It is messier than you anticipated.
4. It requires greater determination than you expected.

The only thing that keeps the Swindolls halfway sane these days is hope. All six of us force ourselves to see the finished dream in our minds . . . and, until then, hang tough. "Some day (we keep repeating) it will all be done." *Tell me it's true!*

A marriage is a lot like our house. While new it sparkles. Fresh smells, fun surprises, and new discoveries make each day snap, crackle, and pop. Sure, there's work to be done, but the newness takes away the hassle. As time passes, however, things change. Slowly, almost imperceptibly, the grit of responsibility mixed with the grind of routine starts to take its toll. Who hasn't experienced it?

Bills come due. Weeds sprout. Doors squeak and sag. Windows stick. Paint peels. Roofs leak. Faucets drip. Drains clog. Floors lose their luster. The fun 'n' games silently erode into relentless, demanding, irritating tasks. The dreams fade into the misty memories of "the way we were," introducing us to nightmarish and fearful feelings of "the way it is."

That warm, passionate fire that once cast its spell upon us is obviously dying down. Thoughts and words once foreign to us now reside in our heads and tumble out of our mouths.

• • •

Suddenly we realize we're faced with a decision: Move out or stay and remodel. Walk away from the embers or rekindle the fire. Too often the first choice is considered the romantic resolve. The honeymoon is over . . . dreams lie broken and scattered . . . there is nothing left of the relationship that once was. The duet has become a duel. The smiles and laughter that once made coming home sheer ecstasy have turned into lonely  stares and sighs of disappointment. The magic is gone. Nothing is left in its place except cold mental mirrors reflecting yesterday's sunshine that today has been eclipsed.

Years ago, I read somewhere that getting married is like buying an album of music. You really like one side of the record, but you have to take the flip side with it. Right now, however, you feel like all you've got is the hole in the middle! Gone are those romantic strings with their magnetic melodies of a lingering embrace, kisses of reassurance, and quiet evenings of treasured pleasure. Instead of caring-and-listening communication, you get busy signals . . . and you do not know how to repair the lines.

Enter the advice of others:

> "Look, you don't have to keep torturing yourself. Bail out! Life's too short to spend it in a losing battle. You've given it your best shot and it hasn't worked—so, give it up. Or the least you can do is try an exciting affair. Get a little fun back into your life. There are lots of available and attractive lovers with no strings attached. We're not living in the 1920s anymore! Things are a lot different now. Love today means 'never having to say you're sorry,' not 'I'm stuck with this creep the rest of my life.' And marriage is okay for those who are too insecure to cut it on their own. But you're not the type. Why stay in

• • •

that miserable cage? You are free! Walk away and never look back—everybody's doing it."

This is no exaggeration. And every year the assault is greater. Heavy verbal artillery pounds away at weak marriages and the fragile strings that hold many homes together. With relentless and merciless regularity, those screaming shells land with telling blows, leaving the bruised and bloody victims with the choice of digging in or dropping out.

You don't need to be told which option many married couples are choosing today. Chances are good you yourself have entertained the thought of selling out. It's certainly easier to bail out than to work through. At least it seems so at the present time. Remember the four? It takes a lot of time. It's costly. It's just plain messy and painful. It's tough. Toughest thing you can imagine! Furthermore, when we're surrounded by so many "authorities" who say that starting a new fire is so much more exciting than stoking an old one, it's not only tempting, it's downright appealing.

But deep down inside you, there's something tugging at you, urging you to stay at it, to pay the price, to stir up what's there rather than kick aside the charred remains of what was once so enjoyable, so fulfilling. That "something" dare not be ignored! It may very well be the voice of God quietly yet forcefully reminding you of those words:

> . . . with love, I take you,
> . . . for better, for worse,
> . . . 'til death do us part.

That's what this book is all about. It offers a strong challenge. I mean it when I say it's not for babies. It's really designed for you who are willing to get down to business and let the Bible strike the original match as you and your

• • •

partner glean God's timeless truth to help you rekindle that fire. For sure, He will see you through the whole process.

Essentially, this is a biblical book on marriage. You've already found that bookstores—non-Christian and Christian alike—have several shelves bulging with books on marriage. Many offer clear logic and current ideas, some interesting psychology, good philosophy, and even colorful pictures surrounded with amazing stories, fascinating experiences, life-changing testimonies, and moving devotional thoughts. Most are written by qualified people, many of them Christians—good books by good authors who believe in the Good Book—but as I read them, I keep asking, "Where are the Scriptures that support your point?" Or, "That sounds right, but is that a biblical principle or a personal one?"

This volume attempts to fill that gap. I assure you, everything of significant importance will be drawn from the Bible, God's original blueprint for married couples to follow. But this doesn't mean I'm going to preach at you. You will soon discover that these things I share are realistic, believable, positive, nontechnical, and free from perfectionistic demands. Read that sentence again. As I write about marriage, I promise to filter everything through those five checkpoints.

Along with numerous references to the Bible, I frequently mention my own marriage. Not because it's perfect, but because it's the only marriage I really know in depth. Since we began our partnership together on June 18, 1955, Cynthia and I have worked through some extremely difficult times. We have been determined to take God at His Word and do those things which He says *will* work! For almost a quarter of a century (!) we have learned how to survive and flex, grow and forgive, using the very same principles I men-

• • •

tion in this book. They are too good, too valuable, too necessary to keep to ourselves.

With the addition of four active children (two teenagers, two soon to be), we've put these things to the acid test. *They work.* If they didn't, I would never waste your time or mine. Ours is a home occupied by six sinners, plain and simple. We live with all the built-in hazards that could lead to fractured relationships and collapsed bridges of communication. Life in this Southern California zoo is life in the raw, friends and neighbors. If a marriage can stay strong out here, those principles being used need to be passed around. Our only claim is God's abounding grace that enables us to change in some area almost every day so that harmony might prevail as we keep rekindling the fire.

If we can do it, anybody can. And that includes you. Admittedly, it's lengthy, costly, messy, and hard work. But it's not impossible. When you consider the alternative, it's well worth all the time and effort involved.

● ● ●

# 1
...

# *Let's Consult the Architect*

*T*HE AMERICAN FAMILY is in trouble. Bad trouble. Marriages are hurting, even Christian marriages. Strangely, the happily married couple seems an oddity in our times. This is true even among those we once admired.

An executive from one of my publishers visited me several months ago. En route to the West Coast, he made several overnight stops, hoping to make contact with potential authors. When we met for dinner, he was obviously more somber than I had ever seen him. As I probed he responded.

"Chuck, on my way out here I made six stops, each in a major metropolitan area of our nation. At each place I either heard about or dealt with influential, once-respected Christian statesmen—solid evangelicals, men committed to the truths of Scripture—who have left their wives."

• • •

Shocked, I asked if these individuals seemed broken . . . if they felt they had done everything possible to hold their homes together. I will never forget his answer.

"Broken? No way! As a matter of fact, most men left their wives for another woman . . . and they are still engaged in the Christian ministry as if nothing ever happened."

It is this new dimension of an old problem that has prompted me, more than anything else, to write a book on marriage. Unhappy marriages, domestic conflicts, and spiraling divorce rates have always been among us. For years people have been asking, "Is it realistic and right to enforce a 50-year contract on a 20-year-old couple?" Wives and husbands alike have walked away from one another for decades. A "permanent marriage bond" has never been a unanimous American opinion. Especially among non-Christian people. The sign that hung in the Hollywood jewelry store window for several months some time ago didn't even make front-page news in the *Los Angeles Times*:

WE RENT WEDDING RINGS.

So what's the big deal . . . *in the world system.*

There is a new wrinkle, however, that troubles me in all this. This temporary commitment to marriage is now being embraced by many Christians. Frankly, I'm a little surprised when I see a happily married, non-Christian couple. I'll tell you, they're pulling off an amazing feat! On the sheer force of human ingenuity and man-made determination, they are hanging in there. But the Christian couple?

Listen, we have the power and presence of the living Lord available to us, the prayer support of others in the family of God, the inner-working of the Holy Spirit, plus the divinely-inspired handbook of instruction on  marriage and the home

● ● ●

... not to mention pastoral instruction week after week, marriage and family conferences, and helpful books and tapes on the subject. Our cup is abundantly full and running over.

In spite of all those resources, Christian husbands and wives are walking away. Willfully. Openly. Unashamedly. In many cases, free of any twinge of guilt or the slightest fear of God. I'll tell you, we have come upon an unusual era. It is difficult enough to exist in the smog of troubled and broken marriages among the unsaved world ... but now that the same syndrome is floating into the Christian family, it's time to get involved in some effort that can turn the tide.

We need to blow the dust off God's original blueprint for marriage and the home. Our great need is to hear what He has to say to His people about His design. After all, marriage is His invention. It's obvious that He understands it best, since He holds the patent on it. As the Master Architect, the Lord is the most qualified authority, so we seek His counsel first and foremost. Let's hear what He has to say about His invention.

## A "Good" Reason for a Relationship

It is in the second chapter of Genesis that we find the first detailed reference to the first man and woman. Theologians refer to such scriptures as a "passage of primary reference." If we expect to grasp God's viewpoint of the marriage relationship, an understanding of Genesis 2:18–25 is crucial.

> Then the Lord God said, "It is not good for the man to be alone; I will make him a helper suitable for him."
> And out of the ground the Lord God formed every beast of the field and every bird of the sky, and brought them to the man to see what he would call them; and

• • •

whatever the man called a living creature, that was its
name.

And the man gave names to all the cattle, and to the
birds of the sky, and to every beast of the field, but for
Adam there was not found a helper suitable for him.

So the Lord God caused a deep sleep to fall upon the
man, and he slept; then He took one of his ribs, and
closed up the flesh at that place.

And the Lord God fashioned into a woman the rib
which He had taken from the man, and brought her to
the man.

And the man said, "This is now bone of my bones,
and flesh of my flesh; she shall be called Woman, because
she was taken out of Man."

For this cause a man shall leave his father and his
mother, and shall cleave to his wife; and they shall
become one flesh.

And the man and his wife were both naked and were
not ashamed.

This event occurred on the sixth day of the creative week.
God performed miracle after miracle, day after day. On four
distinct occasions He passed His approval on His creation.

> . . . God saw that it was good (1:12).
> . . . God saw that it was good (1:18).
> . . . God saw that it was good (1:21).
> . . . God saw all that He had made, and behold, it was
> very good (1:31).

But what do you notice about God's statement regarding
Adam in Genesis 2:18?

> . . . it is not good. . . .

This is the first time in all the Bible that God says something is *not* good. What is *not* good? God declares it isn't

● ● ●

good for man to be alone. This isn't just a passing comment. In the original Hebrew, the language in which the Old Testament was written, the negative is most emphatic; therefore, it appears first in the phrase. Literally it says, "Not good, is man's aloneness. . . ." God, the Creator, saw man, His creature, in an isolated, alone-condition. He announced that Adam's solitary state was not good. God cared about Adam's "aloneness."

I will never forget performing a wedding for a couple who had been engaged for about two years—quite a long while when you're in love. The groom was as anxious as any man I've ever seen. During my preliminary, introductory comments in the ceremony, I chose to read this verse—Genesis 2:18. No sooner had I explained the emphatic statement, "not good, is man's aloneness," than the nervous groom sounded forth a stage whisper you could hear in a little theater off Broadway: "*AMEN!* " Who knows? Maybe Adam did the same. Being all alone, living an isolated, lonely life is hard to bear, something troubled partners tend to forget as they contemplate divorce.

## Aloneness Answered

But the Creator did more than declare a problem. He announced the solution:

> "I will make him a helper suitable for him."

We'll look at these verses more in depth in Chapter 2. But for the moment, notice the first title God gave the woman: *helper.* Our English word doesn't sound very important. In fact, my latest copy of Webster's New Collegiate Dictionary sets forth this definition:

• • •

> helper *n.*: one that helps; *esp.*: a relatively unskilled
> worker who assists a skilled worker, usu. by man-
> ual labor[1]

Wow, in this day of aggressive feminists, them's fightin words! The Hebrew, however, is much more meaningful. It conveys the idea of someone who "assists another to reach complete fulfillment." It is used elsewhere in the Old Testament when referring to someone coming to rescue another. God's answer to man's lonely existence was a woman . . . one who would be there to be a vital part of his finding fulfillment, one to rescue him.

And if that isn't vivid enough, God adds that the one He would bring alongside Adam would be "suitable for him." Literally, "corresponding to" him. She would provide those missing pieces from the puzzle of his life. She would complete him as a qualified, corresponding partner. It is a beautiful picture of a dignified, necessary role filled by one whom God would make and bring alongside the man. In God's original design the plan was to have each partner distinct and unique, needing each other and therefore finding fulfillment with each other.

### God Gives Away the Bride

After predicting, God performed. He made the woman from man's rib. Listen to the account:

> So the Lord God caused a deep sleep to fall upon the
> man, and he slept; then He took one of his ribs, and
> closed up the flesh at that place.
> And the Lord God fashioned into a woman the rib
> which He had taken from the man, and brought her to
> the man (2:21, 22).

• • •

What a fabulous scene! The term "fashioned" means "to build, to rebuild so as to cause to flourish." God rebuilt that rib so uniquely that the thing came to life. It "flourished" into a lovely creature . . . Adam's God-given partner.

It then says that God "brought her to the man." After which, Adam exclaimed, "This is it!" *(Living Bible).* Today the groom would say, "Right on! All right, that's the one!" Adam realized she had been made by God, given to him by God, and designed especially for his needs. Small wonder we read of his excitement.

This is a tender, touching scene. You and your wife would do well to relive it and put it into today's language and needs. Mutual respect must somehow be restored. It is in that context that love flourishes. In God's original blueprint we find the woman needed by the man, significant to the man, and even honored alongside the man. We also see the man finding completeness and fulfillment, neither of which were possible without the woman. Transparently, he exclaims "This is it!" As if to say, "She's the one!" Openly, he declares his gratitude.

I am especially impressed with the fact that God *personally* brought that particular person to Adam. What a thought! Your marriage will turn a vital corner when you realize that it is the Lord who personally prepared your mate for you. No doubt you have different temperaments, different interests, different perspectives, tastes, abilities, personalities, and moods. It is these differences that add variety and color to your marriage.

I was well over ten years into our marriage before I became aware of the value of this principle, that is, being grateful for the differences between my wife and me. For over a decade I resented it, I now admit to my embarrass-

• • •

ment. I was often irritated that she didn't view things exactly as I viewed them . . . that she frequently represented
another side of an issue . . . you know, another opinion than
mine. It wasn't that she was argumentative (I often was!) but
only expressive of her honest feelings. She approached a situation differently than I, she saw other shades of meaning,
she had other feelings. I took that as a lack of submission
and told her so. Time and again we locked horns until finally God showed me from this "passage of primary reference"
that my wife was different because *he had made her different.* She was all the more valuable to me because of those
differences. She was not designed to be my echo, a little
vanilla shadow curled up in a corner, awaiting my next
order. She was designed by God to be my counterpart, a necessary and needed individual to help me become all God
wanted me to be.

## Four "Musts" for Marriages

Now, back to these last two verses in Genesis 2.

> For this cause a man shall leave his father and his
> mother, and shall cleave to his wife; and they shall
> become one flesh.
> And the man and his wife were both naked and were
> not ashamed.

Take a few extra seconds to read those words again—slowly
and thoughtfully, preferably aloud. You'll observe an
absence of quotation marks—indicating these words were
probably not a part of the original dialogue between God
and Adam. Observe also the mention of father and mother.
Obviously, these verses have a much broader scope than
Adam and Eve, for the original couple had neither father nor
mother. I suggest that many years later God gave Moses (the

• • •

one who wrote Genesis) these thoughts to record as guidelines for all marriages throughout time. They stand as the earliest definitive statement ever made regarding marriage.

Having meditated on these words for an extended period of time, I want to offer four foundational guidelines for a meaningful marriage. Each term is related to a portion of these two verses. You might want to put them in the margin of your Bible.

| | |
|---|---|
| . . . a man shall leave his father and mother | SEVERANCE |
| . . . and shall cleave to his wife | PERMANENCE |
| . . . and they shall become one flesh | UNITY |
| . . . and the man and his wife were both naked and were not ashamed. | INTIMACY |

Without wanting to oversimplify marital conflicts and complications, I can say that in most every difficulty I've dealt with, one or more of these guidelines were either ignored or violated. They are basic to domestic harmony. I state that unequivocally so you will take them seriously. Chances are good that if you do so, you will begin to find the right combination that opens the vault leading to some answers you've been looking for. Because they are so important, I will postpone our probing into each until the next chapter.

Before doing so, however, let me warn you against approaching these guidelines in a mechanical manner. In other words, try not to view these things as "four steps to absolute marital harmony," like an airtight, magic formula. They must be blended with *wisdom, understanding,* and *knowledge.* Without these three vital ingredients, all attempts at rekindling the fire that once kept your marriage warm will fail.

• • •

### Changing the Floor Plan

Turn to Proverbs 24:3–4. Take the time to ponder these words Solomon wrote centuries ago:

> By wisdom a house is built,
> And by understanding it is established;
> And by knowledge the rooms are filled
> With all precious and pleasant riches.

The writer offers dependable counsel regarding the home. He is not referring to material things, such as matching drapes and carpet, a two-car garage, or a new sofa. No, these verses say the real answer does not rest in what we possess but in what we are. Your marriage will not be restored because you buy the right things but because you become the right one. These two verses don't even mention people. A home is built by wisdom . . . its structure is established by understanding . . . its rooms are enriched by knowledge.

Look at the verbs: built, established, filled. They are words that suggest action, progress, change, aren't they? The first word, "built," comes from the Hebrew term meaning "to restore." It's the idea of rebuilding something so that it flourishes. It's the same word we just read in Genesis 2 where God took Adam's rib from his chest and "rebuilt" the bony substance into Eve. The point Solomon is making is clear. Any home can be restored, rebuilt. It is never too late. But it isn't automatic. Wisdom is needed. We'll think more about that in a moment.

"Established" means "to set in order, to place in an erect or upright position" something that is falling or twisted. Understanding is needed for this.

Third, each room is "filled," meaning "overflowing," and the idea includes fulfillment, abundant satisfaction. Knowl-

• • •

edge makes that happen. The "precious and pleasant riches" mentioned here have nothing to do with tangible possessions—but rather the essential things that make life full and meaningful. Things like positive attitudes, good relationships, pleasant memories, mutual respect, depth of character. The things that cannot be destroyed even though your home may burn to the ground.

I first taught these truths about the essentials for life in our church in Fullerton and I tried to make the point clear with an illustration. I suggested that everyone imagine driving home from church that Sunday afternoon, turning the corner that leads to their street—then suddenly realizing as they turned into their driveway that their house had burned down to the foundation. Nothing remained except a naked brick fireplace and the concrete slab covered with smoldering chunks of wood. I added that even though such a calamity might occur, none of the "precious and pleasant riches" would have been destroyed. You cannot burn memories or relationships. Fire can't destroy character or attitudes.

Tape recordings were made of those messages on marriage. They now reach around the world. Three years later I received a letter from a woman who had heard the tape with that illustration. Listen to her words:

Dear Pastor Swindoll:

Two years ago I was hosting a weekly Bible study in our home. We had selected a series of your tapes to study, and while listening, one of your messages sunk deep into my heart. . . .

You were speaking on storing our treasures in heaven. You asked the question, "What would you do if you drove into your driveway and found a pile of ashes?"

• • •

That question really got me, as I had a houseful of three generations of antiques which I had restored. These "things" were my roots, reminding me of loving memories of grandparents.

Well, six months later I drove in my driveway and found our two-story home in a pile of glowing red ashes. I really praised the Lord for so lovingly preparing me six months prior by hearing your message on tape. . . .

I instantly knew that I hadn't really lost a thing. . . .

Remarkable. And so true. No tragedy can destroy the things that make a marriage strong.

You see, a major mistake is being made in our day. Couples are working overtime to purchase things, to add more gadgets and conveniences and elaborate appointments to their houses. But those things don't satisfy. They soon fade and fail.

## The Three Vital Ingredients

God says we need only three essential ingredients to restore our marriage and make it flourish again. They are:

*Wisdom.* Seeing with discernment. It's having a broad perspective. The term stresses accuracy, the ability to sense that which is beneath the surface. Wisdom doesn't skate.

*Understanding.* Responding with insight. Establishing your marriage calls for this ingredient. As I view something with discernment (from God's perspective), I am better equipped to respond with insight, not to take it personally or feel the need to fight back.

*Knowledge.* Learning with perception. It includes having a teachable spirit, a willingness to hear, a desire to discover. Knowledge includes taking the time and going to the trouble

● ● ●

to learn. Growing, healthy mates are in constant pursuit of the truth.

Let's put these two verses back together into an amplified paraphrase.

> By means of wisdom—the skill to see with discernment, maintaining a broad yet accurate view of life—a house is rebuilt, restored so that those within it don't simply exist, they flourish, they reach their full potential. By means of understanding—the ability to respond with insight, gaining a full awareness of situations that results in an insightful response rather than a surface reaction—one brings order and an upright condition back to a marriage and home.
>
> By means of knowledge—the willingness to learn with perception, becoming acquainted with the facts and grasping their significance so that ignorance is dispelled and truth is continually pursued—one causes each life to be filled to overflowing with riches that can never be destroyed, like memories, positive attitudes, mutual respect, and a depth of character.

Now you see why I warned you against becoming "mechanical" as if operating with a magic-formula mind-set. Now you see why I wanted to come to terms with these essentials before going into the four guidelines in Genesis 2:24–25. To implement each guideline will require wisdom, understanding, and knowledge. You simply cannot crank out four quick little principles and suddenly expect your marriage to blossom.

## It Can't Be Done!

No doubt, you're asking *how?* How can I gain wisdom and understanding and knowledge? The answer is not a list

● ● ●

of dos and don'ts, believe me. Nor can you get them from some book or seminar or by traveling to some location in the world where these things are dispensed. The answer, again, is in the Bible. Turn to Proverbs 2:6.

> For the Lord gives wisdom;
> From His mouth come knowledge and understanding.

A companion verse is Psalm 127:1:

> Unless the Lord builds the house,
> They labor in vain who build it;
> Unless the Lord guards the city,
> The watchman keeps awake in vain.

The Lord alone can give you these skills and abilities. You can't do it on your own. Working independently of Him will accomplish zero. Frustration and futility will haunt you if you try to do it in your own strength. Remember, it is the *Lord* who gives these gifts. Unless the *Lord* pulls it off, you labor in vain. This means you need to be a Christian . . . and you need to turn to Him regularly. I'll spell out some practical hints in the pages that follow; but, at the bottom line, only the Lord can give you these three essential ingredients. Remember, marriage is *His* invention. He holds the patent.

The time to start is *now*. Remember Adam? God stepped in and said, "Not good!" Face the music. Declare your need. Start today.

The method to follow is *God's*. No need to run down to the city library and check out five or six books. They will disagree and you'll be confused. God's method is direct and to the point. Follow His instructions.

The person to change is *you*. Not your mate. Not your circumstance. With wisdom, understanding, and knowledge,

• • •

you can experience a whole new frame of mind. You can actually be fulfilled in spite of less-than-ideal circumstances. The person to focus on all through this book is you.

Charlie Shedd was right. "Marriage . . . is not so much finding the right person as it is *being* the right person."[2] I want to talk about that in the next chapter. Better take a deep breath before you dig into it, however. It may hurt. Normally, you have to blast before you can build.

If you're willing, then start with me at ground level. Let's repair the foundation.

### Notes

1. *Webster's New Collegiate Dictionary,* s.v. "helper," © 1980 by G. & C. Merriam Co.

2. Charles W. Shedd, *Letters to Karen* (Nashville: Abingdon Press, 1965), p. 13.

● ● ●

# 2
...

## Let's Repair the Foundation

*I*T WAS ON ONE OF THOSE television talk shows several months ago. The guest was an actor, well-known for his romantic roles on film. Predictably, he was asked, "What makes a great lover?" I am confident everyone watching the show (myself included) expected the standard macho-playboy response. To the surprise of the host and the audience, his answer must have raised eyebrows all across America. It went something like this:

> "A great lover is someone who can satisfy one woman all her life long . . . and who can be satisfied by one woman all his life long. A great lover is not someone who goes from woman to woman to woman. Any dog can do that."

• • •

Wow! May his tribe increase. Unfortunately, our actor friend is outnumbered by many more so-called authorities on the subject of marriage. A war is raging, in fact. It is a shouting war waged in the press and movies, on TV screens and lecture platforms, among college students and angry women's liberationists, and in today's reading material. Hardly a week passes without our hearing that marriage represses and degrades women. Believing this to be true, universities from Maine to California have now added to the curriculum courses offering information on alternatives to marriage, declaring that the age-old family concepts are in transition, soon to be replaced with domestic options for the nuclear age.

Is the war real or theoretical? Has the bombardment been effective? According to a survey of student opinion conducted by Daniel Yankelovich, Inc., in 1971, the number of students who believed that marriage is obsolete was increasing substantially. The results showed an alarming 24 percent. By May, 1971, it had leaped to 34 percent, one out of every three![1] And that survey, remember, was a decade old in 1981. No, the war on marriage is certainly not theoretical. And even if you are genuinely committed to your mate, you cannot keep from suffering somewhat from the fallout and flak that splatters across our society.

In the previous chapter, we learned from Genesis 2 that the God who created man and woman also invented the way they could live in harmony with each another. Likewise, we gleaned from Proverbs 24:3–4 three truths to help us find fulfillment in our marriage: wisdom, understanding, and knowledge. Without these at work in our relationship, we will lack the protection from enemy attack as our own marriage will be weakened and ultimately lose its fire.

• • •

Let's reread Genesis 2:24–25, that "passage of primary reference," and dig deeper into those early guidelines the Lord gave Adam and Eve. Remember, now, they are for *all* marriages, not just the first one. This is verified by the fact that Jesus, many centuries later, returned to the Genesis 2 account when answering a question regarding divorce (Matthew 19:4–5). Paul did the same when he addressed the subject of marriage in Ephesians 5:22–33. These guidelines are timeless and as relevant and dependable today as the first day God gave them. Although ancient, familiar, and reliable, they are nevertheless continually ignored.

### Severance

The first directive God declared was:

> For this cause a man shall leave his father and his
> mother. . . .

In order for the new relationship between bride and groom to flourish and their home to begin correctly, the cord must be cut with the parents. This does not mean abandoning our parents or ignoring or mistreating or cutting off all contact with them. To "leave father and mother" means to break the parent-child bond, to sever the tight, emotionally dependent strings that once provided security, protection, financial assistance, and physical needs. All or any of those ties, if brought over into a marriage, will hinder the bond of marriage from sealing. So God mentions this first, even before He talks about "cleaving" to each other.

This is sound advice for parents to heed just as much as it is for those getting married. Release your child! That is perhaps the best wedding gift you can give. Ideally, verbalize your willingness to sever those ties. I know of some parents

● ● ●

who actually wrote their feelings and decision on a piece of paper, giving it to the bride and groom on the wedding day. Good idea!

More and more I am including the parents in the wedding ceremony, asking them to stand and publicly agree to release their parental authority and entrust their offspring to the new home beginning that day. This, I believe, cements the decision and makes it permanent in everyone's mind. Newly married couples need that freedom before they are able to give themselves fully to one another.

Severance must permanently impact the bride and groom as well. Leaving father and mother is a painful, difficult decision for some. In fact, it keeps many a person from cultivating a serious relationship with the opposite sex. I smile every time I hear the American folk song, *Billy Boy.* Maybe you didn't learn all the lyrics, so you never discovered why Billy Boy and his girlfriend didn't marry. When you sing, "She's a young thing and cannot leave her mother," you get the impression she was twelve or thirteen . . . or certainly not over fifteen. Right? Wrong! Listen to the stanza:

> How old is she, Billy Boy, Billy Boy?
> How old is she, charming Billy?
> Three times six and four times sev'n,
> Twenty eight and elev'n,
> She's a young thing and cannot leave her mother.[2]

Can you believe that? Billy Boy's girlfriend was 85 years old! Makes one wonder how old her *mother* was. But all along, she was viewed as "a young thing and cannot leave her mother." That old folk song contains a common misconception.

Severance is basic to a healthy marriage. May I add one

• • •

final thought along this line? Your husband is your husband, not "daddy," wife. Your wife is your wife, not "momma," husband. No matter how many children God gives you . . . no matter how long you may have been married, calling each other "mother" and "daddy" can take its toll on your romantic feelings for each other. You leave father and mother . . . you don't marry them!

### Permanence

In order for a marriage to survive the war, each couple needs to view the commitment to each other as an irrevocable, permanent bond. Read the verse again:

> For this cause a man shall leave . . . and cleave to his
> wife. . . .

Leave and cleave. Sever and bond. Loosen and secure. Depart from and attach to. The Hebrew term, translated "cleave" means "to glue, to cling." Moses writes of diseases "clinging" to the body. Job mentions bones "clinging" to the skin. Both use this same original word.

Today's problem is largely explained by the fact that couples enter the marriage relationship believing it is terminable. "Till death do us part" is, unfortunately, a mere verbal formality to many who utter those words. The whole concept of establishing a permanent bond between a husband and a wife is quickly becoming a foreign thought. More and more it is being interpreted, "Till disagreement do us part" or "Till other interests do us part." It was never meant to be so in God's original match.

Cynthia and I, for several years now, have determined to strengthen our relationship by declaring our permanent commitment to each other. This is something we took for grant-

• • •

ed far too long. It is no longer something we assume. Periodically, through the year (especially on New Year's Day, our anniversary, and each other's birthday), we affirm our commitment, eyeball to eyeball, stating our love and devotion to each other. This really helps! We do not consider separation even an option, no matter how hot the disagreement—and, believe me, it gets awfully hot at times. This is all part of cleaving to each other. Regardless of the difficulty or the problem we are working through, the bond God sealed in June, 1955, is not ours to break.

During England's darkest days in the late 1930s and early 1940s, it was a pudgy, cigar-smoking, unimpressive-looking man who held the country together. While other voices were shouting, *"Surrender!"*—Sir Winston Churchill stood fast. Bombs devastated city blocks, buildings crumbled, bridges fell, but the stubborn Prime Minister refused to budge. Never once did he consider capitulating or even negotiating with the Nazis. He operated on a rather simple rule of thumb when it came to winning a war. On numerous occasions Churchill stated his philosophy in six words:

"Wars are not won by evacuations!"

Surrendering is not an option if you plan to win a war . . . or succeed in a marriage. I firmly agree with that San Francisco attorney I heard in a meeting some time ago, "There are two processes that must never be started prematurely: embalming and divorce."

Severance from dad and mom is first. Permanence between husband and wife is next. Third is . . .

## Unity

Listen to these words once more:

● ● ●

> For this cause a man shall leave his father and his
> mother, and shall cleave to his wife; and they shall
> become one flesh.

It's the last part that interests us. Becoming one flesh suggests a process, not an instant fact. Two people with different backgrounds, temperaments, habits, scars, feelings, parents, educational pursuits, gifts, and interests don't immediately leave a wedding ceremony in perfect unity. The process *begins* there, however. And it is a lifelong project requiring wisdom, understanding, and knowledge.

Unity is not to be misconstrued as uniformity. God brought Eve to Adam . . . not to be a female Adam but to be distinctly unique, obviously different from him. Uniformity occurs in donut shops as bakers punch out their pastries. It happens in Detroit as long assembly lines crank out Chevys. It is essential in a Marine boot camp as young men are squeezed into the same mold. But that is not what God had in mind when He stated that the two would become one flesh.

The whole idea of mutual acceptance, giving, listening, forgiving, belonging, and direction was implied. It is two individuals willingly blending into each other's lives, desiring to share with and thereby complete the other. Read Paul's words along this line:

> Let the husband fulfill his duty to his wife, and like-
> wise also the wife to her husband.
> The wife does not have authority over her own body,
> but the husband does; and likewise also the husband
> does not have authority over his own body, but the wife
> does.
>
> 1 CORINTHIANS 7:3–4

• • •

The picture is one of total unselfishness, two persons actively engaged in "fulfilling" his/her duty . . . to the partner. How rare today!

The following statements were taken from a suggested "Marriage Contract" I heard about from a friend who had read about it in some secular magazine.

> I will not give come on signals to others for sexual relations when I see that you feel threatened . . . we are separate people with our own standards and they must never be fused into one . . . I cannot make you happy or unhappy, but I can make myself happy . . . I accept my ultimate aloneness and responsibility for myself.

What a joke! I ask you, where's the unity?

Few people are able to express this concept of unity better than the late Peter Marshall. He described marital harmony this way:

> Marriage is not a federation of two sovereign states.
> It is a union—
> domestic
>   social
>     spiritual
>       physical.
>
> It is a fusion of two hearts—
>   the union of two lives—
>     the coming together of two tributaries,
> which, after being joined in marriage, will flow
> in the same channel
>   in the same direction . . .
> carrying the same burdens of responsibility and
> obligation.[3]

• • •

Rekindling your marriage fire calls for a severance from parents, a permanence in the seal, a growing unity as two become one and . . .

## Intimacy

Take time to consider the order of things as God reveals these timeless guidelines. Surrounded by the security of commitment to each other, the acceptance brought on only by mutual respect and love, and an undeniable unity of purpose and goals . . . the joys of personal intimacy are not only present, they *flourish*. That explains why

> . . . the man and his wife were both naked and were
> not ashamed.

This guideline of intimacy is mentioned last in God's foundational list. There's a reason, though. The delights of intimacy between a husband and his wife are enjoyed because severance, permanence, and unity are obviously in operation. Remove the context of these other three foundational pillars and *whoosh,* intimacy quickly disappears.

Before I describe how this facet of intimacy in marriage is being twisted today, let me probe deeper into Genesis 2:25. The Hebrew term translated "naked" suggests the idea "laid bare," emphasizing totally and completely naked. When the verse adds that Adam and Eve "were not ashamed," the idea from the original construction is reciprocal—they weren't ashamed "before or with one another." Amplified, the picture is they had no hidden areas, no hang-ups, no embarrassment, no fears. There was total transparency, the complete absence of self-consciousness. This gave them unrestrained freedom. Emotionally as well as physically. Inwardly and outwardly.

• • •

The absence of sin allowed such unhindered ecstasy. I find it exceedingly significant that in the very next chapter of Genesis, when sin entered into their lives, Adam and Eve immediately covered up. And for the first time, they admitted an awareness of their own nakedness. Listen to Genesis 3:9–10.

> Then the Lord God called to the man, and said to him, "Where are you?"
> And he said, "I heard the sound of Thee in the garden, and I was afraid because I was naked; so I hid myself."

Why the cover-up? "I was afraid . . . so I hid myself." for the first time in *all* of time, mankind became self-conscious. Up to that point, each was so totally involved in the other (thanks to their sinless condition) it never dawned on them that they were naked. Their unguarded transparency prompted unrestrained intimacy with each other. That was exactly as God originally meant it to be.

How different today! Crippled, diseased, and blinded by the pollution of sin, people wrestle desperately to relate freely and openly. The same is true of marriage partners. Intimacy, therefore, often becomes a frustrating struggle, a strange mixture of selfishness, embarrassment, dissatisfaction, and resentment . . . with only brief glimpses of pleasure and fulfillment. Because this subject is somewhat complex, I have reserved an entire chapter in which we can come to terms with the major issues—Chapter 5.

Some, of course, think an answer to sexual frustration is in having an affair or two . . . or three. The grass always looks greener, doesn't it? It certainly seems easier. Instead of cultivating and acquiring the skills of intimacy (yes, there are definite *skills* involved in lovemaking), extramarital

● ● ●

escapades seems to offer the ecstasies of pleasure without the agonies of responsibilities.

Right? Well, you decide after reading this. My good friend, Joyce Landorf, is appreciated as an author because she tells it straight. *Tough and Tender,* one of her many best-sellers, is no exception. In that excellent chapter, "The Gentle Lover," she mentions a man she calls George, who used to work at her husband's (Dick) bank. George's recent divorce led him into the swinging scene of sexual liberation. If anybody ever looked like the most enviable California bachelor in banking, George certainly did. A beach apartment. Beauty queens in and out. No-hassle sex night after night. The guy had it made. Or did he?

Listen to the flip side.

> . . . one afternoon George came up to my husband's desk and haltingly said. "Uh, Dick, could I talk to you about something?"
>
> Then, as nearly as Dick can remember, this is what George related. "You know, Dick, I've really got it made. I'm free from the attachments of marriage. I've got this great pad at the beach and I go to bed with one sexy gal after another. I come and go as I please and I do my own thing. But something is really bothering me and I can't figure it out. Every morning as I get dressed for work I look into the mirror and I think 'What was last night's sexy little game all about? Sure the girl was good-looking. She was good in bed and she left this morning without bugging me, but is that all there is in life?' I asked myself, 'If this life style is what every guy thinks he wants, why am I so depressed? Why do I feel a cold nothingness all the time?'"

• • •

He stopped, leaned closer to Dick and quietly continued. "I know the guys here think it would be fantastic to have this kind of liberated freedom but honestly, Dick, I hate this life." He sat back and paused for a few seconds and then wistfully added. "You know what I'd really like? I'd like to go home tonight, smell dinner cooking, hug my wife hello, and spend the evening telling her and showing her how much I love her. I'd like to go to bed with her and not have to prove my virility, not have to sexually perform above the call of duty, but just give her love, and go to sleep knowing she'd be there in the morning."[4]

There it is, my friend. Straight scoop from an honest guy. Intimacy, fulfilling, enjoyable, meaningful intimacy must emerge from the God-ordained context of commitment and acceptance and marital harmony. That's all part of His arrangement. The original design cannot be improved upon, even though the propaganda sings another tune. Dance to that strange music, and believe me, you'll pay the piper. And he's expensive.

Well, there they are:

severance
   permanence
      unity
         intimacy

Foundational guidelines upon which everything rests. And the tools needed to construct the project?

wisdom
   understanding
      knowledge

● ● ●

Being ingenious, man will fiddle around with the original design and make changes. Erasing this, rearranging that, taking out, adding to . . . until it scarcely resembles what the Lord God created. And the result? Just look around. Listen to the media. Check the courtroom. Read the latest stuff. You won't see much resemblance.

The Christian Medical Society offers its helpful journal to our generation. It is both relevant and insightful. Several months ago the issue was dedicated to the problem of divorce. Included in the publication was an article lifted from *The Washington Post* entitled "Open Marriage . . . Broken Marriage."

> "Open Marriage," by George and Nena O'Neill, was a book for the times and it said over and over again that you should be honest, straight, out-front, give space, let the other person do their thing, communicate and if you wanted to have an affair, for God's sake, do be honest about it—don't sneak around, make excuses, call late in the afternoon with some cock-and-bull story about work. Simply pick up the phone and say, "Honey, I'll be a bit late tonight. I'm going to have an affair."
>
> But there were these couples I know. They were open. They were honest. They were having affairs. They were not sneaking around (applause), they were not lying (applause), they were being honest (whistles). They were being open. Everyone agreed that it was wonderful. The men agreed and the women agreed and I agreed and it all made you wonder. Then they split. There was something wrong. Invariably, someone couldn't take it. It has nothing to do with the head. The head understood. It was the heart; it was, you should pardon the expression, broken.

● ● ●

It all made you think. It made you think that maybe there are things we still don't know about men and women and maybe before we spit in the eye of tradition we ought to know what we're doing. I have some theories and one of them is that one of the ways you measure love is not with words, but with actions—with commitment, with what you are willing to give up, with what you are willing to share with no one else.[5]

Whether Richard Cohen, the one who wrote that, is a Christian or not, I cannot say. But he's got his finger on the pulse of the problem. Maybe you see yourself in the mirror of his message. Perhaps some things are becoming increasingly more clear to you. Possibly God is breaking through those years and showing you that your marriage is shaky because a poor foundation was poured.

Don't be afraid to say so. Admission of a problem is the first step toward solving it. And it's often a *giant* step. If you're willing to repair the foundation, then you shouldn't have too much difficulty choosing the bricks that will help rebuild your marriage.

## Notes

1. Lester Velie, "The War on the American Family," *Reader's Digest,* January 1973, pp. 106–110.

2. "Billy Boy," *Folk Songs for Everyone* (New York: Remick Music Corporation, 1962), p. 54.

3. Catherine Marshall, *A Man Called Peter* (Lincoln, Va.: Chosen Books, 1951), p. 54.

4. Joyce Landorf, *Tough and Tender* (Old Tappan, New Jersey: Fleming H. Revell Company, 1975), pp. 132–133.

5. Richard Cohen, "Open Marriage . . . Broken Marriage," *The Washington Post,* © 1977 and reprinted by permission.

• • •

# 3
...

# Bricks That Build a Marriage

FOUR-YEAR-OLD SUZIE had just been told the story of "Snow White" for the first time in her life. She could hardly wait to get home from nursery school to tell her mommy. With wide-eyed excitement, she retold the fairy tale to her mother that afternoon. After relating how Prince Charming had arrived on his beautiful white horse and kissed Snow White back to life, Suzie asked loudly:

"And do you know what happened then?"

"Yes," said her mom, "they lived happily ever after."

"No," responded Suzie, with a frown, ". . . they got married."

In childlike innocence, that little nursery schooler spoke the in-depth truth without realizing it. Getting married and living happily ever after are not necessarily synonymous.

• • •

Check the stats, if you're not convinced. "The American Family" was one of the feature articles in a national periodical some time ago. It was enlightening, informative . . . and depressing. Especially the grim graph that revealed the growing divorce rate. Hang on. In 1960, there were 25 divorces for every 100 marriages in America. In 1975, the rate jumped to 48 divorces per 100 marriages. The article stated that at the present rate of increase, there will be 63 divorces for every 100 marriages by 1990.[1] In case you haven't a calculator handy, that's an increase of 150 percent in one generation. Happily ever after? Not quite.

We are learning that a major factor in this growing problem is that couples have departed from God's original design. His blueprint has either been changed or ignored altogether. The foundation He planned has not been poured correctly. So it isn't surprising the construction fails to pass the test of time. Repairs are costly and time-consuming . . . but that's the only way. And as the process of restoration transpires, hope and encouragement return.

Remember what we uncovered earlier from Proverbs 24:3–4?

> By wisdom a house is built,
> And by understanding it is established;
> And by knowledge the rooms are filled
> With all precious and pleasant riches.

A marriage *can* be rebuilt by "wisdom." It *can* be set in order by "understanding." It *can* actually be filled with indestructible things that no calamity can remove and no thief can steal. That takes "knowledge." I want to keep reminding you of those three ingredients, lest you think that rebuilding your house into a home is simply a brick-and-mortar proposition. A sensitive, insightful spirit, a responsive, positive

• • •

attitude, a teachable, willing heart are bottom-line essentials for a marriage. Keep that on the front burner, for sure.

But there are some practical building materials God has ordered for His design. We're told about these materials— these bricks—in letters from Paul and Peter in the New Testament. (When I was preparing this chapter and realized we were going to get the counsel of Paul and Peter, I was tempted to entitle it "Peter, Paul, and Marriage.") In Ephesians 5 Paul gives us the pattern for the overall structure, the superstructure. In 1 Peter 3, Peter specifies the bricks along with the mortar to bond them together.

## A Superstructure That Supports

No one can claim he has done a thoroughly biblical study of marriage without dealing with Ephesians 5:22–33. In these verses, Paul first speaks to wives (vv. 22–24) and then to husbands (vv. 25–33). In both sections there is a basic role declared and then an analogy to emphasize the significance of the role.

*Wives*   Paul writes:

> Wives, be subject to your own husbands, as to the Lord.
> For the husband is the head of the wife, as Christ also is the head of the church, He Himself being the Savior of the body.
> But as the church is subject to Christ, so also the wives ought to be to their husbands in everything.

It doesn't take a Greek scholar to see that Paul gives a command, "Wives, be subject to your own husbands . . . " and then a comparison . . . "as to the Lord." For wives, the basic role is one of submission, and the analogy is "as to the

● ● ●

Lord." As the Christian wife would respond to her Lord, so she is to do to her husband.

### Husbands    Paul adds:

> Husbands, love your wives, just as Christ also loved
> the church and gave Himself up for her;

Again, it isn't complicated. The husband's basic role is adoration . . . and the analogy is ". . . as Christ also loved the church and gave Himself up for her."

Both roles have unique patterns and both are analogous to Jesus Christ. The godly wife asks, "Lord, how can I show my love to You in the role you have called me to fill?" God answers, "My dear child, show it in your submissive heart toward your husband." The godly husband asks, "Lord, how can I be the kind of man you want me to be as a husband?" God answers, "My son, your limitless love for your wife shows the world and shows Me the kind of love you have for Me."

### Two Questions    Tucked away within the seams of these verses are two implied yet penetrating questions each partner needs to ask. The wife must come to terms with her role and ask, "Do I love my husband enough to *live* for him?" And, equally important, the husband must come to terms with his role and ask, "Do I love my wife enough to *die* for her?" Searching questions. But they put the issues in the right perspective.

The world today doesn't talk about a husband loving his wife enough to die for her. Mention that idea on any TV talk show and listen for the razz-ma-tazz from host and audience alike. And drop the word "submission" on them if you really

• • •

want to wake them up—submission of the wife, that is. Immediately, you'll be categorized as some ignorant weirdo who believes in slave chambers of torture and one who promotes chaining women in a washroom. The very idea! I mean, what thinking person today can possibly imagine squashing a woman under the heels of a man . . . or shoving her in corner, reducing her activities to changing diapers, doing dishes, checking off a grocery list, and mopping floors?

Strange, isn't it, how angry and misinformed individuals invariably envision that kind of stuff whenever submission is mentioned. Everytime I hear it I know the person simply doesn't understand the biblical teaching on submission. When placed in the right setting (wisdom, understanding, knowledge), the woman's worth is *enhanced* and her life is *enriched* by a husband who adores her. There is, in that context, fulfillment and freedom rarely experienced elsewhere on earth.

Yes, I'm realistic enough to know that there will always be some who take advantage of their roles. Husbands who crack the whip because they are "in charge" . . . wives who manipulate and maneuver, using "submissive techniques" they learned from their mothers or other women. This brings incredible pressures into a home. Like this letter I received after I spoke on marriage and the family in our church:

> This series on marriage! Oh, God! How I need it!
> How we need it—Joe (not his real name) and I. If these
> folks around us only knew . . . but praise God, they
> don't. It's somehow easier to hide behind this facade—to
> play the game our friends expect of us while the struggle
> merely to "hang in" strains and stretches the last feeble
> threads of the web.

● ● ●

These things Paul and Peter are proposing—I've tried them again and again and again, but it's hard, God. You know me and Joe. Last Sunday, we were hardly home from church when Joe began to stoke up the management of the home role. All week, he had been away on business and I had maintained meals and schedules and a certain semblance of comfort and balance. But, now it's Mighty Joe Christian, manager of the home, telling the kids they don't have to eat their meat loaf, that they will take naps, that my son can't wear his new tee-shirt, and casting a reproachful look at me when my spirit inevitably erodes with neither gentleness nor control. Of course, it's an effort for him, too, to insist that the children thank me for a not-that-great pancake dinner in the evening and not call attention to the fact that he's helping with the dishes. And God, only You know what it must cost this man behind closed doors to continue to offer a gift that is not wanted.

But I'm here, Lord, warts and all, and so is Joe and the threads, though warped and worn, that have kept these volatile energies from spinning off into parallel orbits long ago. Can it be, Lord, that these threads can become strands in ropes and cables, if even one of us sells out wall-to-wall for Jesus Christ? We were so sure of that once!

. . . Oh, one more thing, Lord! . . . if it's all the same, could you start with Joe??. . . and the meat loaf??

Even though wrongs are committed and unfair advantages are taken, God's overall structure still stands. What we often need is some practical help on how to pull it off. Paul has given us that "what." Peter gives us help with the "how." Paul explains the structure, the underlying frame. Peter

● ● ●

shows us the actual bricks that give the marriage color and beauty.

## Bricks That Build

In the first nine verses of 1 Peter 3, there are practical suggestions for the wife (vv. 1–6), the husband (v. 7), and a brief wrap-up (vv. 8–9).

Take the time to read all nine verses slowly and thoughtfully.

> In the same way, you wives, be submissive to your own husbands so that even if any of them are disobedient to the word, they may be won without a word by the behavior of their wives,
>
> as they observe your chaste and respectful behavior.
>
> And let not your adornment be merely external—braiding the hair, and wearing gold jewelry, or putting on dresses;
>
> but let it be the hidden person of the heart, with the imperishable quality of a gentle and quiet spirit, which is precious in the sight of God.
>
> For in this way in former times the holy women also, who hoped in God, used to adorn themselves, being submissive to their own husbands.
>
> Thus Sarah obeyed Abraham, calling him lord, and you have become her children if you do what is right without being frightened by any fear.
>
> You husbands likewise, live with your wives in an understanding way, as with a weaker vessel, since she is a woman; and grant her honor as a fellow-heir of the grace of life, so that your prayers may not be hindered. To sum up, let all be harmonious, sympathetic, brotherly, kindhearted, and humble in spirit;

● ● ●

not returning evil for evil or insult for insult, but giving a blessing instead; for you were called for the very
purpose that you might inherit a blessing.

**Bricks for Wives**  I'm confident some of you wives are thinking, "Sure, I will be glad to live like that as long as I have the
right kind of husband." But these verses are written especially
to the wife who has the *wrong* kind of husband. If that's your
situation these four bricks are molded just for you.

**The Brick Entitled "Behavior"**  First, God talks about your
*behavior.* The scene Peter paints is a familiar one. Ornery
husband, raspy response, irritable temperament. But even
though the guy is tough to live with, he isn't blind! He cannot ignore the behavior of his godly wife. That's what ultimately "wins" him. And the way it happens is not through
little notes pinned to his pillow or elbow nudges in church.
He "observes" your behavior.

Interesting term. It is the Greek word for a careful observation, a close look, like sports fans watching an instant
replay of some close call. That reminds me of what once
happened during the NFL playoffs a couple years ago. Being
the avid football fan I am, I have managed to infect our older
son, Curt, with the same disease. He and I follow the game
with fanatic interest, especially when the Dallas Cowboys
are playing.

All season long (and for some wives, it's *really* long), we
had watched the season run its course. The Cowboys and the
Rams were slugging it out for the next playoff berth. A judgment call was made by the ref and just as the instant replay
began to review the action in slow motion. Cynthia snapped
on the vacuum cleaner and started in on the den where we

• • •

were sitting. I couldn't believe it! Curt and I were on the edge of our chairs staring, studying the call . . . and in comes Mrs. Tidy with that suction snorkel and the sound of a cotton gin.

I shouted, "What in the world are you doing, Cynthia?" Without looking up, she said, "I'm cleaning the stadium!" Don't get me wrong. She enjoys football too . . . but after four-plus months of it, the place does begin to resemble box seats at the Rose Bowl.

It's what my son and I were doing that applies to this second verse. We were not casually glancing at the replay. We were absorbed in it, focusing full attention on it. That's what husbands ultimately do when their wives' "chaste and respectful behavior" is consistently on display. It's what one man calls, "the silent preaching of a lovely life."[2]

**The Brick Labeled "Appearance"**  The second "brick" that helps build a stronger marriage is the wife's *appearance*.

> And let not your adornment be merely external—
> braiding the hair, and wearing gold jewelry, or putting
> on dresses;
>     but let it be the hidden person of the heart, with the
> imperishable quality of a gentle and quiet spirit, which is
> precious in the sight of God.

Let's focus in on the main thrust of this passage. Peter's point is clear. You are warned against *going overboard*, patching up the externals if your internals are pitifully lacking. Don't place all your emphasis on the outside . . . but, on the other hand, this doesn't mean there *shouldn't* be something on the outside worth looking at.

I've heard preachers run wild with these verses. "Braiding the hair"—you see, you mustn't braid your hair, they say.

• • •

"Wearing gold jewelry"—skip the accessories, they insist. It's carnal. But the verse also mentions "putting on dresses." Funny thing, I've never heard a preacher encourage nudity . . . but if he presses his forced logic, that's next.

Listen, this passage isn't bad-mouthing cosmetics or taking shots at keeping yourself physically attractive, ladies. It's just encouraging you to *keep it in balance.* Not external only, remember. Some wives need all the help they can get! Like the old saying, "If the house needs painting, *paint it.*" Good advice for wives, too. It's a shame some have not learned the importance of keeping themselves attractive. All day long their husbands encounter fantastic women, well-dressed and appealing, and what do they see when they walk in the kitchen at 5:30 p.m.? The totaled woman.

What's the difference? The importance of appearance. A man doesn't stay interested in a wife who smells like she just got dipped in Lysol. Or runs around the house looking like an unmade bed all day. For sure, you need to be pure within . . . but don't stop when you get to the outside. There's no reason in the world a Christian woman can't look attractive just as often as possible. Whatever it takes, do it! Your appearance is a significant "brick" that helps rebuild a marriage.

***The Brick Called "Attitude"*** There's a third: *attitude.* Look at verses 3 and 4 again.

> And let not your adornment be merely external—braiding the hair, and wearing gold jewelry, or putting on dresses;
> but let it be the hidden person of the heart, with the imperishable quality of a gentle and quiet spirit, which is precious in the sight of God.

• • •

The phrase, "hidden person of the heart," is a New Testament description of the wife's attitude. And what characteristic in her attitude does God consider important? He mentions specifically ". . . the imperishable quality of a gentle and quiet spirit. . . ." What a beautiful expression! God views a gentle and quiet spirit as *imperishable.* And He adds that it is "precious in the sight of God." The word "precious" is from the same Greek term Peter used earlier when referring to imperishable "faith" (1:7) and the imperishable "blood" of our Lord Jesus Christ (1:19). Wives, your attitude is *that* important. It cannot be erased or passed over or destroyed.

"But I'm not gentle and quiet. God didn't make me mousey," say some of you ladies who read this. As in the case of submission mentioned earlier in the chapter, this attitude is misunderstood by many who read it. It's not a reference to being weak or a female doormat. Actually, these are terms that speak of strength of character, strong self-control, a person of quiet elegance and dignity.

One of my wife's favorite Bible verses is hidden away in the last chapter of Proverbs. It is in a context of other verses describing the "excellent wife" (v. 10). After stating how rare and capable she is, how worthy of her husband's trust, and how respected in the eyes of others, the writer drops this additional comment:

> Strength and dignity are her clothing,
> And she smiles at the future (31:25).

It's a picture of unusual beauty. She is inwardly clothed with strength of character and confidence. She isn't shallow or loud or cheap. She's got class, we would say.

Being "gentle and quiet" is another way of saying "tranquil and under control." Does that sound like weakness?

• • •

Those who are in control of themselves and free from panic or irritation are people of amazing strength. Small wonder the one who wrote Proverbs 31 asks,

> An excellent wife, who can find?

When Peter uses the term, "gentle," he has in mind genuine humility, one who does not fight against either God or others. It is an absence of struggle and contention. "Quiet" indicates "tranquility arising from within, causing no disturbance to others."[3] This kind of wife isn't churning within or restless without.

Before leaving this third character "brick," I want to add that it takes only a little while to doll up the externals (important though that may be), but cultivating "the hidden person of the heart" is a lifetime process.

This was emphasized to me in an unforgettable manner as I was driving on one of our Southern California freeways some time ago. Right in front of me that morning were a husband and wife apparently driving to work together. As he drove, she dressed! I'm not kidding. She had hopped in with everything she needed to wear . . . and she worked feverishly during that twenty-five-minute ride putting it on. Including eyelashes and earrings right down to heels and hose. The drive was the only R-rated trip I've ever made. Yep, in twenty-five minutes a woman can perform a minor miracle from the skin out . . . but her "hidden person"? Ah, that's the task of a lifetime.

***The Brick Designated "Response"*** We've covered three "bricks" thus far: behavior, appearance, and attitude. We need one more to complete the pattern for the wife: *response*. Verses 5 and 6 form the basis:

• • •

> For in this way in former times the holy women also, who hoped in God, used to adorn themselves, being submissive to their own husbands.
>
> Thus Sarah obeyed Abraham, calling him lord, and you have become her children if you do what is right without being frightened by any fear.

Before your feathers get ruffled by what this says of Sarah ("obeyed"), it will help you to realize the Greek verb means "to pay close attention to" someone. It's the idea of attending to the needs of another. A positive, helpful response is written between these lines.

Wives, please listen closely. If you are the energetic type, your tendency will be to dash all over the globe, responding to the needs of people everywhere. Clubs, classes, and courses will clamor for your time. And unless you're careful, they'll get it. If not all of it, *most* of it. Even church stuff will occupy every hour you'll give. Some of you have become far more concerned about responding to others' needs outside the home than to that one individual most important to you within the home.

I can't fathom Sarah's leaving this note pinned to their tent one evening as Abraham shuffled home from work, bone-tired and dangerously hungry:

Abe:

> Mutton pot pie in the stone oven. Gone to Torah study with the ladies at Bethel. Took the small chariot. Be home late. Don't worry. Be sure to give Ishmael herbs for cough at sundown. And bathe Isaac.

SARAH

> P.S. Don't forget to close all the flaps when you go to bed. Sandstorm is coming.

• • •

Some of you think, "If I start being as responsive as you suggest, my husband will take advantage of me. He'll walk all over me. Give him an inch and he takes a mile." You need to look at the last part of verse 6 again.

> . . . do what is right without being frightened by any fear.

There's your promise. God will honor your loving and supportive response, ladies. Relax. He won't allow your mate to stomp all over your gracious response. It's a brick, remember. It's solid and strong. It hurts when you stomp on bricks.

**Bricks for Husbands**   I've been tossing some tough bricks on the wives. I warned you, ladies, remodeling is hard work. But now, let's see what God says to the man of the house. It is equally potent.

> You husbands likewise, live with your wives in an understanding way, as with a weaker vessel, since she is a woman; and grant her honor as a fellow-heir of the grace of life, so that your prayers may not be hindered.

**A First Brick**   The first brick for the husband is obvious: *Live with your wife.* "Hey, I do! Come home every night. We have the same address, eat at the same table, sleep in the same bed, and even use the same bathroom." But that's not all this verse is talking about. The original term translated "live" means "to dwell down," and it suggests being closely aligned, being completely at home with. The little word "with" is a term calling for close companionship, deep-down togetherness.

Many a husband looks to the wife to maintain this. "My job's the office, her job's the home. I earn the bucks, she

● ● ●

handles the bills. The business is mine and all its headaches. The home is hers and all those needs related to it." That may be the way you were raised, my friend, but it isn't the way God originally designed it for husbands. No way. On the front end of everything the Lord says in this verse, "living with your wife" is paramount. It is our task to lay the groundwork for domestic harmony, husbands. We are the ones who should be cultivating an in-depth partnership with our mates. We are to initiate the action, encourage the process.

Cynthia and I came across this truth many years ago. It began to haunt me that I was becoming much more passive (like my own father) in matters pertaining to the home. I was leaving more and more decisions up to her, unconsciously turning over the reins of leadership. It was *convenient,* frankly. I could always use the excuse of pressures related to the church I was serving or demands on my time from people in great need for spiritual counsel. It was also a lot *easier.* Being the hot-shot down at the church was a downhill slide in comparison to the nitty-gritty leadership of the home. It was much more glamorous, far more ego-satisfying, and certainly "more spiritual" to care for the flock as a shepherd than establish and embellish a partnership with my wife.

Then God shot a right jab to my jaw with 1 Timothy 3:4–5, where He writes to pastors who are also husbands:

> He must be one who manages his own household
> well, keeping his children under control with all dignity
> (but if a man does not know how to manage his own
> household, how will he take care of the church of God?);

• • •

See the word "manage"? It's mentioned twice. It means, literally, "to preside over, to lead," but it's much broader. Listen to this excellent explanation:

> A good manager knows how to put other people to work. . . . He will be careful not to neglect or destroy his wife's abilities. Rather, he will use them to the fullest. . . . He does not consider her someone to be dragged along. Rather, he thinks of her as a useful, helpful, and wonderful blessing from God. . . .
>
> A manager has an eye focused on all that is happening in his house, but he does not do everything himself. Instead, he looks at the whole picture and keeps everything under control. He knows everything that is going on, how it is operating, and only when it is necessary to do so steps in to change and to modify or in some way to help.[4]

That really convicted me! Since making the discovery and implementing some changes, I have traveled to one seminary and Bible school after another underscoring the importance of the home life of the minister. Not infrequently, it is the *first* time many of the men have ever considered the vital link between their relationship with their wives and families and the congregations they serve.

It is absolutely imperative, men, that we fight our tendency to be passive in matters pertaining to the home. The passive husband continues to be one of the most common complaints I hear from troubled homes. Men, *get with it!* Your wife will grow in her respect for you as soon as she sees your desire to take the leadership and management of the home.

• • •

*A Second Brick*  A second "brick" for husbands could be put in these words: *Know your wife.* Again, this might sound like something you are already doing. The original expression, however, will help you determine if you are. Literally, the expression means "dwell together according to knowledge." The success of your dwelling with your wife, my friend, will be in direct proportion to your knowledge of her.

Knowing your wife includes those things about her that others don't and won't know. Her deep fears and cares. Her disappointments as well as her expectations. Her scars and secrets and also her thoughts and dreams. That's *knowing* your wife. It calls for a sensitive spirit, a willingness to be involved, to listen, to communicate, to care. Husbands—if your marriage is eroding this is one of the most important issues you can give yourself to. It will do as much to heal her hurts and calm the storm as anything I could suggest. Your wife longs to be understood and to know you desire that.

*A Third Brick*  Finally, Peter says *honor your wife.*

> . . . and grant her honor as a fellow-heir of the grace of life.

The term rendered "grant" means "to assign" and here the husband "assigns" her a place of honor. Interestingly, the term "honor" and the previously used word "precious" are from the same Greek root. Husband, what place have you "assigned" your wife? Maybe you really value her and appreciate her. It's quite likely you genuinely view her as a precious treasure, a person you might esteem, you honor.

Does *she* know it? Have you told her? Do you demonstrate that honor you claim to have for her? Guys like us tend to assume our wives know how much they mean to us.

• • •

But there is nothing like telling her. Sometimes with well-chosen words. Other times with flowers. With small, elegant gifts. With letters we mail to them while we're away. With little notes here and there. With a meal for two at one of her favorite spots. With a surprise weekend trip where new surroundings and room service and relaxing around a pool offer undeniable proof that she is significant and worth a lot to you. On the way back home, believe me, your wife won't have as much difficulty believing that you really *want* to be close to her, to know her, to honor her.

## Beginning Construction

Need a place to start? Here's how. Reserve an evening soon, preferably this week. You can stay home or take a drive or go to dinner or spend the night somewhere special. The place isn't as important as the project, but you do need to be alone so you can think and talk and respond without interruption.

1. Spend at least fifteen minutes in silence, thinking about and writing down the four things you appreciate the most about your mate. Husbands, you talk first for a change. Both listen carefully.

2. Using 1 Peter 3:1–7 as your guide, admit the one trait or habit you would most like to see the Lord change in your life. Declare your desire to cooperate with His changing you.

3. Before going to bed, set at least two major goals for your marriage. Pray together and ask God to make them a reality rather than simply a distant dream.

4. After both finish, give the list of four areas of appreciation to each other. Keep it and review it several times that evening and during the week that follows.

• • •

If you haven't done this for a long time (for some of you—*ever!*), it will seem awkward and maybe even a little embarrassing. Handling bricks is a skill that has to be learned, you know. But once you get the hang of it, once you get hold of authentic communication, open and unguarded sharing, no substitute will do.

Fake bricks never are as attractive or valuable as the real thing. So watch out for cheap substitutes.

## Notes

1. The Reporter's Notes, "Family Trends Now Taking Shape," *U.S. News & World Report,* October 27, 1975, p. 32. Material taken from the copyrighted chart, "Divorce: More and More Common."

2. William Barclay, "The Letters of James and Peter" in *The Daily Study Bible* (Edinburgh: The Saint Andrew Press, 1976), p. 219.

3. W. E. Vine, *An Expository Dictionary of New Testament Words,* 4 vols. (Old Tappan, New Jersey: Fleming H. Revell Company, 1940), 3:242.

4. Jay E. Adams, *Christian Living in the Home* (Grand Rapids: Baker Book House, 1972), pp. 91–92.

● ● ●

# 4

...

# Watch Out for Cheap Substitutes!

WE ARE LIVING IN A DAY of synthetics. Imitations, counterfeits, and artificials abound. They fit our plastic world, unfortunately.

Let's face it, we've grown accustomed to cheap substitutes. Vinyl has virtually taken the place of genuine leather. Formica looks almost like wood. Artificial flowers "bloom" year-round. Substitute foods, synthetic fabrics, man-made lakes, rocks, and trees have become so perfected they are actually preferred by many. The phony appears so real, you have to examine closely or you'll be fooled. But when you get down to the details, when you really pay attention, it is obvious why the authentic is better. And when the bottom line is drawn, the genuine is always more valuable than any substitute.

Maybe you heard about the guy who fell in love with an

• • •

opera singer. He hardly knew her, since his only view of the singer was through binoculars—from the third balcony. But he was convinced he could live "happily ever after" married to a voice like that. He scarcely noticed she was considerably older than he. Nor did he care that she walked with a limp. Her mezzo-soprano voice would take them through whatever might come. After a whirlwind romance and a hurry-up ceremony, they were off for their honeymoon together.

She began to prepare for their first night together. As he watched, his chin dropped to his chest. She plucked out her glass eye and plopped it into a container on the nightstand. She pulled off her wig, ripped off her false eyelashes, yanked out her dentures, unstrapped her artificial leg, and smiled at him as she slipped off her glasses that hid her hearing aid. Stunned and horrified, he gasped, "For goodness sake, woman, *sing, sing, SING!*"

In this chapter we're thinking about a different set of substitutes . . . but they are nevertheless just as damaging to a marriage. In fact, more so. We're thinking about things that are put on the outside to cover up what's missing on the inside. Cheap substitutes that wives and husbands are tempted to use instead of genuine qualities that make a marriage strong and stable.

## Substitutes Wives Often Use

In the same passage that gave us helpful guidelines to strengthen a marriage (1 Peter 3:1–9), we find some warnings against cheap substitutes. Wives, because these verses start with you, so will I. In verses 1 through 6, there are three substitutes that wives often use. If you're ready, let's roll up our sleeves and dig in.

• • •

*Scheming in Secret*  The first substitute is *secret manipulation*. Listen to the first two verses, ladies:

> In the same way, you wives, be submissive to your own husbands so that even if any of them are disobedient to the word, they may be won without a word by the behavior of their wives,
> as they observe your chaste and respectful behavior.
>
> 1 PETER 3:1–2

Because we've already examined these words rather closely, there is no reason to do that again. But it will be helpful if you will observe these verses call for a quiet spirit, a wife who is characterized by control and tranquility—in spite of a disruptive home situation kept in turmoil by a disobedient husband. God says, "Let Me handle your man. You leave the preaching to Me. What I want from you is a godly life. Remember, he won't be able to ignore your quiet, calm spirit." But that's tough! And because it is, many wives resort to a substitute for this quiet spirit. They employ a technique I will call secret manipulation.

Webster says that manipulation means "to control or play upon by unfair or insidious means, especially to one's own advantage or to serve one's own purpose." In other words, secret manipulation is an unfair, insidious technique that results in getting what one wants. When handled cleverly, a wife can substitute secret manipulation for a quiet, submissive spirit.

It's been my observation that the woman who employs this substitute is usually the one who cannot leave things in the hands of God. She finds it virtually impossible to believe that the Lord can handle her husband without her help. Therefore, she resorts to any number of manipulative techniques . . . like moodiness, pouting, sulking, scheming, sexu-

● ● ●

al bargaining, or even lying—even though she would call it "altering the truth just a little." By manipulating her man, she hopes (ultimately) to get her own way. Unfortunately, she usually does. Manipulation works!

A classic illustration of this is Isaac's wife Rebekah. Determined to get her husband to see things her way and to pass special favors and family blessings on to Jacob (her favorite) rather than the first-born Esau, Rebekah manipulated her husband. She led a secret conspiracy and encouraged a scheme that was so effective, Jacob literally tricked his dad into the plan. Genesis 27 tells the tragic story. The deed stands as an ugly, dark splotch on Rebekah's biography.

No amount of rationalization will *ever* justify manipulation, wives. Your husband cannot be manipulated into any permanent change. You may scheme and pressurize him into surrendering to your will. If you are especially good at this, you may develop just the right technique to weaken his resistance and fall into your trap . . . but *it will not glorify God.* In doing so, you will lose more than you will gain. Manipulation weakens a marriage.

Peter's counsel is wise: "without a word." Apart from schemes. Free from manipulation. Trust in the Lord your God to handle your husband. Believe me, He can!

**Unattractive Adornment**    There is a second substitute. It is the strong temptation to substitute *external appeal for internal beauty.* I wrote a little about this in the previous chapter, but more needs to be said. Before that, however, let's read 1 Peter 3:3–4 once again:

> And let not your adornment be merely external—
> braiding the hair, and wearing gold jewelry, or putting
> on dresses;

• • •

but let it be the hidden person of the heart, with the imperishable quality of a gentle and quiet spirit, which is precious in the sight of God.

Remember now, the Scripture is not saying externals are totally unimportant . . . but that externals are not as important as internals. Wives, your physical appearance is indeed significant. The warning here is that it not be your primary focus or emphasis. Being subjected to the relentless bombardment of the media, you will have difficulty keeping this proper scale of priorities. Such pressure will strongly tempt you to substitute a beautiful body, attractive clothing, and exquisite accessories for the lack of quality within. God says—"Don't do it!"

Cecil Osborne refers to the woman who possesses this overemphasis on the externals as a "narcissistic woman." She is one who . . .

> . . . has an inordinate self-love. She is unduly preoccupied with her face, her body, and often with her own interests, which she perceives as an extension of herself. . . .
>
> A man married to a narcissistic woman is in for trouble. If the world does not continue to praise her, and if he does not cater to her infantile whims, she may develop any number of physical or emotional symptoms. . . .
>
> A narcissistic woman constantly seeks to be the center of attention. She seeks flattery and is engaged in constant battle for popularity. She is sometimes a "psychic scalp collector," flirting with men in order to prove to herself that she has not lost her attractiveness. She uses men, including her husband.[1]

● ● ●

For the woman who genuinely wants to be a godly wife, my advice is to give greater attention to your inner person—those "imperishable qualities"—than to your physical attractiveness. In the long run, believe me, your husband will be much more satisfied and stimulated over your inner beauty.

***Learning Rather Than Doing***  Let me mention one more "cheap substitute" so common among Christian wives in our day, before addressing the husbands. It is *learning about what's right rather than doing what is right.*

Listen to Peter's counsel once again:

> For in this way in former times the holy women also, who hoped in God, used to adorn themselves, being submissive to their own husbands.
>
> Thus Sarah obeyed Abraham, calling him lord, and you have become her children if you do what is right without being frightened by any fear.
>
> I PETER 3:5–6

Those verses mention how modern-day wives can become "Sarah's children" (i.e., a woman like Sarah) and emulate the life style she modeled. How? Look very closely at the verses:

> . . . if you do what is right. . . .

It has been my observation that a large percentage of Christian wives know more—much more—than they put into practice. And yet, they are continually interested in attending another class, taking another course, reading another book, going to another seminar . . . learning, discussing, studying, discovering more and more and more. And what results? Normally, greater guilt. Or, on the other

● ● ●

side, an enormous backlog of theoretical data that blinds and thickens the conscience rather than spurs it into action. Learning more truth is a poor and cheap substitute for stopping and putting into action the truth already learned.

Christian wife, stop and think. Please. Think about your goals, your deep-down desires as a wife. More than likely, they are commendable, probably as pure as Sarah's in ancient days. Next, think about your role. Is it clear? Is it understood? Probably so. Now then . . . in order to carry out your goals and fulfill your role, do you need to learn more or start doing what you already know is right?

Please understand, I am not against seminars and feminars, courses and clubs, books and Bible studies. But it troubles me to see the same women year after year dashing to class after class instead of concentrating full and uninterrupted attention on *doing the things they've learned.*

At the risk of being misunderstood, ladies, I plead with you! Take an honest, objective look at your marriage. In all candor, do you really need more facts, more principles, or more classes this year? How about backing off and digging in? Why not take a personal sabbatical from so many activities and concentrate your full, undivided attention on your husband and your home. For sure, some people won't understand. But on the other hand, you will reap some amazing and rewarding dividends.

I am acquainted with a wife and mother of several children. She was engaged in a hectic schedule of appointments, meetings, committees, and responsibilities. All of them were good, necessary functions and closely connected with her church or related Christian ministries. Her calendar was full as she tried to juggle the car pool, the P.T.A. and other school activities, a few trips out of town with her husband, and sev-

● ● ●

eral evenings of entertainment each month at home. There were meals to fix, lunches to pack, shopping trips, phone calls, sewing needs, and a half dozen other demands. One day she stopped everything. I mean *everything.* She sat alone in a chair at the kitchen table and thought about herself for a change. "What in the world am I doing? Why am I involved in so much? Is *all* this essential, really necessary?"

She faced the hard fact that "the hidden person of her heart" was not a gentle, quiet spirit. She acknowledged before God that her numerous involvements were displeasing to Him (and her husband, I might add). She prayed. She openly confessed her sin of substituting activity for application. She wept aloud as all this broke into her conscious realization.

The result? She canceled every possible thing she could so the essentials might take first place for a change. Her husband was beside himself with delight. Even her children expressed gratitude to her within a week. She told me recently she soon came to realize that much of the stuff she was "learning" was not actually being absorbed at all. She now finds herself genuinely enthusiastic about her role, her home, and her future.

Cheap substitutes are, nevertheless, strong-willed and persuasive. They're like the battery—they die hard. But by God's power they can be cast aside. Through Him, you remove those cheap substitutes of secret manipulation, an overemphasis on the externals, and the tendency to hectically keep learning, going, and running instead of simply doing what is right.

## Substitutes Husbands Often Use

Now let's look at the flip side of the same record. The zoom lens of Scripture focuses now on the husband.

● ● ●

> You husbands likewise, live with your wives in an
> understanding way, as with a weaker vessel, since she is a
> woman; and grant her honor as a fellow heir of the grace
> of life, so that your prayers may not be hindered.
>
> 1 PETER 3:7

From this single verse, I find three more "cheap substitutes." These are the ones men frequently use in their marriage.

***Enter Provider . . . Exit Lover***   The first substitute is *providing a living instead of sharing a life.* One of the most common misconceptions husbands have goes something like this:

"Now that I have worked hard and provided you with a nice place, sufficient food, and the clothes you need, what more could you ask of me?"

If the guy is a Christian and likes to support his comment with verses of Scripture, he is sure to use 1 Timothy 5:8:

> But if any one does not provide for his own, and especially for those of his household, he has denied the faith, and is worse than an unbeliever.

Enter hard-working, diligent, self-satisfied, smug husband:

"My wife has so much more than most, she has no reason whatever to gripe!"

But wait, husbands. Your wife married *you*, not your paycheck. Of course, it's commendable that you take care of her physical and obvious needs. If you recall, you promised to do that back when you two were married. But the tendency on our part as husbands is to substitute providing for our wives in place of sharing our personal lives with them.

Recently, I buried a 42-year-old woman from our church, a fine Christian wife and mother. Beside that fresh grave the

• • •

husband leaned on my shoulder and wept loudly. He sobbed as he spoke.

"I gave her everything but myself. I gave her things . . . but I didn't give her my time, my attention, my ear to listen as she spoke."

I'm honest, it's at times like that God speaks to me as well. His words hang in my head like a heavy weight. Do they convict you, too?

Peter's counsel is clear:

> . . . live with your wives in an understanding way. . . .
> . . . be considerate as you live with your wives. . . .
>
> (NIV)

The Greek term translated "live" suggests being "at home with." Many a wife is lonely for her husband to sense and minister to her inner spirit. To give her his attention and personal presence. She waits to be noticed, to be appreciated, to be given time to share and, in return, to hear her husband respond.

With the newspaper laid aside.

With the television off.

With the whole evening available.

Men, maybe it will help to motivate you if you face the fact that a continually absent husband is a major cause for illicit affairs among wives. And often with other men who will simply give them time and attention. Wake up, husbands! Sharing your life cannot be replaced with providing nice things. I challenge you to set aside a block of time every day . . . and at least one evening every week for your wife. You cannot imagine the benefits until you actually start that habit.

• • •

*The Intimidator*  Another substitute relates to the man's leadership. Verse 7 exhorts husbands to live with their wives "in an understanding way, as with a weaker vessel, since she is a woman. . . ." God's Word warns us against *demanding instead of managing.* The male—especially the insecure male—tends to use force and intimidation, demanding certain things of his wife. The verse clearly states that of the two, the wife is the weaker partner. She is like a delicate vessel, deeply in need of being understood. Rare is the husband who spends time and thought coming to an understanding of his wife's needs so he can provide wise management as the leader in his home. Biblical management. Wholesome, positive, helpful management.

One reputable authority turns to 1 Timothy 3:4–5 and writes about being a good manager of one's home.

> The husband's job is to manage his family. That is the best translation of the word proistemi. The idea is "to preside over." The picture is of one who has control but does not do everything by himself. As the elder is to be a manager of a congregation, so the husband is to be a manager of his home. A good manager knows how to get other people to do things. He knows how to spot, develop, and use the gifts of others. That is what a manager is and that is what a husband is to be.

> The husband as the head of the home is its manager. He is the head; the head does not do the work of the body. The husband is not to answer every question or think every thought for his wife—exactly not that. Rather, he is to recognize that God gave him a wife to be a helper. A good manager will look at his helper and say, "She has certain abilities. If I am going to manage my household well, I must see that every last one of those

● ● ●

gifts is developed and put to use as fully as possible." He
will not want to squash her personality; rather, he will
seek to bring it to the fullest flower.[2]

Leadership like that, husbands, is the kind few wives will
have trouble following. How much better than irksome, irritating demands! I have often said that the husband who
shouts and bullies his way through his marriage, screaming,
"I'm the leader around here!" probably isn't. Leaders are
good managers, first and foremost.

My mind returns to a middle-aged couple whose marriage
flame fluctuates between lukewarm and cool. The husband
is the classic intimidator—strong-willed, stubborn, lacking in
tenderness, and often angry. Those qualities apparently have
not hurt his business. He is successful and respected by his
competitors. In fact, in recent months the business has
expanded . . . doubled in the last three years. Down at the
office his forceful style is somewhere between awesome and
fearful. People jump when he speaks. And his decisions and
demands are not up for discussion. He is the boss, no doubt
about it. But when he comes home, things are not the same.
And he cannot handle it. He has left his wife more than
once.

It's not that his wife is rebellious. Nor is she unwilling to
allow him the leadership of the home. It's his forceful style—
his lack of proper management—that has undercut his role
as the leader. He has a *partnership* with his wife, but he is
unwilling to cultivate the give-and-take such a relationship
requires. He brings home the "Listen, I'm the boss!" complex, and resentment is the result. The man makes demands
of his spouse that are both unwise and unfair. Among them
are bizarre sexual fantasies he expects her to participate in
which make her feel like a cheap prostitute in a brothel. The

● ● ●

intimidator-type husband, by the way, usually has trouble cultivating a meaningful romance with his wife. He lacks the tenderness and care that deeply satisfying intimacy requires.

Husband, don't ignore this counsel! You may be the hot-shot, fearful, decisive, awesome boss at the office, but God says you are to be a good manager, and an understanding partner at home. Intimidation will not help you cultivate a godly, healthy marriage.

*The Great Smother-Up*   There's one more substitute worth our time, men. It emerges from the last  part of verse 7:

> . . . and grant her honor as a fellow heir of the grace
> of life. . . .

It's what I would call substituting *smothering instead of honoring*. Loving and respecting your wife is one thing, but smothering her is another! Giving her a place of honor is both biblical and commendable, but placing her on a shelf, protecting and pampering her (for whatever reason) is neither. She is your wife, not an invalid. Not an untouchable, easily breakable china doll. Capable and competent wives need to be appreciated, for sure. But not idolized.

There's another side to smothering. It often stems from jealousy, which Solomon once said is "cruel as the grave." How true!

I once married a couple whose marriage soon suffered from the straight-jacket of smothering jealousy. The new bride and groom weren't in their home a week before he announced, "There will be no secrets between us—ever! Our marriage will have no closed doors, nothing hidden!" That morning he removed every door in the house except those that led outside. Yes, the bedroom doors, the bathroom

● ● ●

door, the kitchen door. *Every door was gone.* No secrets! That's not honoring, it's smothering. It's ruining an intimate relationship that will flow under normal conditions. Jealous, neurotic smothering is a far cry from genuine respect and honor.

## A Final Checklist

How can a husband or wife tell if he or she is using substitutes? Look at the next two verses in 1 Peter 3:

> To sum up, let all be harmonious, sympathetic, brotherly, kindhearted, and humble in spirit;
> not returning evil for evil, or insult for insult, but giving a blessing instead; for you were called for the very purpose that you might inherit a blessing.

That's an inspired checklist from God. Substitutes disrupt harmony. If there is irritation and disharmony, you are probably substituting. Substituting stops the flow of sympathy; resentment builds up in its place. Kindness ceases and hurts begin. Humility is replaced with selfishness. Insults occur as arguments increase. Ultimately, instead of building up each other, an erosion in the marriage transpires as cheap substitutes finally take their toll.

In my ministry I have married hundreds of couples. But on only two or three occasions do I recall the couple coming back to me and admitting their failure to keep the marriage together. One happens to be the first wedding I ever performed. I confess I was shocked to hear it failed because the bride and groom had so much going for them.

She was a ten-talent gal who was an absolutely beautiful woman, inside and out. Well-educated, widely traveled, and deeply committed to Christ. She had a splendid position as a

● ● ●

nurse. He was a medical doctor, having graduated at the top of his class. He planned to do his residency in the Midwest, so they wished to be married prior to the move. He was also a Christian, genuinely interested in spiritual things.

I lost track of them for almost four years. One day my phone rang. I remembered her voice immediately. She asked if we could talk that afternoon. As I met her at the door of my study, I saw a woman who looked fifteen years older. Through tears she poured out her story. The pressure began to build shortly after they arrived for his residency. He worked inhuman hours . . . and finally became dependent on drugs to continue. He saw less and less of her. Lonely, angry, and confused, she became promiscuous. Both began to fake it. Neither was willing to tell the whole truth. He worked all night, she worked all day. Month after miserable month. Arguments led to stormy fights. The cheap substitutes wore thin. Their lives were marked by spiritual compromise, gross immorality, and a growing disillusionment with life in general. Separation led to divorce.

I'll never forget her words. "As I look back, it all started when we were not honest with each other . . . when we failed to come clean and admit our needs. We substituted being phony for being real."

Here was the choice couple—models of beautiful, wholesome and healthy young Americans—with everything going for them: career, intelligence, money, happiness, and mutual love. But cheap substitutes replaced the treasured, authentic ingredients so vital in a marriage. Ecstasy turned to agony.

Your life may not be as dramatic as that, my friend, but you know exactly where you are right now. Having read this chapter, you have all the information you need to know and deal with your present condition. Reject those cheap substi-

• • •

tutes! Stop tolerating them any longer! Come to terms with your life and your marriage now. Do some serious thinking about *yourself*, for a change. Not your mate. Be honest enough to tell the truth so God can direct you back to His original plan. In doing so He will also help you understand why your honeymoon dreams may have turned into a daily nightmare.

## Notes

1. Cecil Osbourne, *The Art of Understanding Your Mate* (Grand Rapids: Zondervan Publishing House, 1970), pp. 201–203.

2. Jay E. Adams, *Christian Living in the Home* (Grand Rapids: Baker Book House, 1972), pp. 76–77.

● ● ●

# 5
...

# Who Says the Honeymoon Must End?

A HARMONIOUS MARRIAGE requires the continual destruction of myths. Just as fast as Hollywood can crank 'em out, married couples need to be ready to assault and destroy those fantasies!

A major myth of marriage is that it is a blissful, easy-going, relaxing cloud that floats from one restful day to the next. The guy who dreamed that one up should be *shot at dawn.*

On the contrary, a marriage that works requires a constant willingness to surrender rights, incredible unselfishness, and the ability to flex. To get this point across, let's play "let's pretend."

Pretend for the next couple of minutes that you and your mate have planned a trip to Hawaii for your mid-February honeymoon. You anticipate a warm, lazy surf, a sun-

• • •

drenched beach outside your spacious hotel honeymoon suite, and lovely evenings under a clear, star-filled sky and that romantic Honolulu moon. Your expectations heighten as you board that luxurious 747 (first class, of course) and start to wing your way west.

But something strange happens in the air. Somehow the cockpit crew gets their signals crossed—and before you know it your plane lands rather clumsily in the northern section of the Swiss Alps.

Instead of sunshine and a warm ocean breeze, it's subzero weather and an icy blast of freezing wind out of the northeast. Instead of clear, starry skies and white sands washed by a tropical surf, it's eight feet of snow, low clouds, the promise of more snow that night. Everywhere you look, it's bright white. For miles. Instead of good ole' English, they speak another language entirely . . . and instead of a honeymoon suite overlooking the Pacific, it's a small cottage tucked away on a rocky, rugged hillside. And the plane needs repair so you can't leave soon. In fact, you are marooned there until the freeze is over . . . which means at least two months!

Immediately you and your starry-eyed sweetie are forced to make a decision. You can adapt yourselves to the new environment—buy some winter clothes, rent ski gear, throw a few logs in the quaint old fireplace, and flex—*or* you can refuse to change. You can wear swimming trunks and a bikini, walk around barefoot, refuse to learn a few words of the language, and sit grim-faced in a cold, snow-covered cabin staring out the window as the snow falls.

It's really up to you.

If you flex, you can turn a tremendous disappointment into an absolutely delightful and memorable experience.

• • •

Cozy evenings around a crackling fire. Fun times on the slopes. Breathtaking sights high up in the Alps. Wow! Sounds fabulous!

But if you choose to stay with "Plan A," you're in for a bitter, resentful, ugly, uncomfortable marathon of misery. Amazing! The Alps are more beautiful than Hawaii ever will be—especially in February—but for those who stubbornly resist change, *no way*.

Now, back to reality. All of us who are married anticipated a fun-in-the-sun Hawaiian delight . . . but to our surprise, it soon became evident that our marriage would be different than we expected. Welcome to the Alps! And to make matters worse, there was no flight back at the end of winter. The need? It's obvious. I've been saying it all through this book. Change. And I mean *drastic* change! The alternative is disaster. And you don't need to be told that many a couple has opted for that.

Listen, friend. Rekindling and preserving our marriage fire *demands* that we continually adjust, constantly adapt. If not, I promise you an end to the honeymoon almost before it begins. But let's be positive. Let's talk about how to keep the honeymoon from ending.

### A New Name for the Honeymoon

For starters, we need to redefine "honeymoon." You're not going to like my suggestion: *adjustment period*. How unromantic can you get? I mean, who wants to say, "We went to Hawaii for our adjustment period." (Sounds like a quick trip to the chiropractor's office.)

But wait a minute. That's exactly what it is! It's the beginning of a whole new life style. Sure, the honeymoon does include that initial burst of physical intimacy, that period of

● ● ●

passionate ecstacy between the wedding ceremony and the return to life's responsibilities. And it is exceedingly important that such an acquaintance be as free as possible from an abrupt letdown. But basically, it is the first acquaintance with reality that both partners have in their relationship. If a couple begins this adjustment period with all four feet firmly fixed on reality, it's doubtful that they will suffer many sudden disappointments.

## A Honeymoon That Never Ended

But lest I sound like an unromantic zombie that walks around in neutral when it comes to the intimate side of marriage, allow me the rest of the chapter to set the record straight. There is no reason any Christian couple needs to think that enjoying each other physically is a temporary, brief experience limited to a couple of weeks in Hawaii—or the Alps! If I understand correctly the things God says in His Word about marital intimacy, He never intended the sexual pleasures of marriage to end. Never. The Bible certainly implies that. Let me show you what I mean. It may surprise you.

In Chapter 2 we looked closely into Genesis 2:24–25. Once again, here's what that passage says:

> For this cause a man shall leave his father and his
> mother, and shall cleave to his wife; and they shall
> become one flesh.
> And the man and his wife were both naked and were
> not ashamed.

You may recall the meaning of the Hebrew term translated "naked." It is "laid bare." Nothing hidden. The absence of self-consciousness. The original couple had maximum

• • •

freedom with each other. They were unhindered emotionally, allowing them to be uninhibited physically. That is why the Lord reports that they were "not ashamed." The intimate joys of the marriage bed were continually fulfilling to both Adam and Eve. Without restraint. Without shame.

That is exactly as God would have it. Now, there is no word here (or later) where things began to deteriorate between them. Their intimacy apparently did not cool off nor did their love life wane. When God struck the original match, there was a blessed, enjoyable warmth that continued throughout that union.

There are reasons their "honeymoon" never ended. The same reasons can lead to a similar experience today, all things being equal. It is incorrect to assume that original design was unique, a one-time-only relationship God created. No, it was a pattern for others to follow.

### Biblical Principles of Marital Intimacy

Actually, there are certain biblical principles regarding marital intimacy that remain constant to this very day. Unfortunately, those principles have long since been bypassed or ignored. Let's blow the dust away and rediscover them one by one.

I find a total of five principles in Scripture that will help counteract sexual deterioration between husband and wife. All five are supported in the Scriptures. And all five have to do with a more meaningful, intimate relationship between married partners, not just two people living together.

***Intimacy: It Is "Very Good"*** *Intimacy in marriage was created in innocence and declared "very good." Let's go back to* Genesis 1:27–31:

• • •

And God created man in His own image, in the image
of God He created him; male and female He created
them.

And God blessed them; and God said to them, "Be
fruitful and multiply, and fill the earth, and subdue it;
and rule over the fish of the sea and over the birds of the
sky, and over every living thing that moves on the earth."

Then God said, "Behold, I have given you every plant
yielding seed that is on the surface of all the earth, and
every tree which has fruit yielding seed; it shall be food
for you;

and to every beast of the earth and to every bird of the
sky and to every thing that moves on the earth which has
life, I have given every green plant for food"; and it was
so.

And God saw all that He had made, and behold, it
was very good.

Take careful note of those last two words: "very good."
Including what? Everything. And that includes, of course,
the sexual delights of marriage. God personally and caringly
created the human body so that it might be stimulated,
aroused, and able to enjoy to the fullest, in marriage, the
complete expression of sexual delight.

I begin here because this is basic. Thinking correctly about
marital intimacy lays the groundwork for enjoying it fully. A
fulfilling experience in bed begins with right thinking in the
head, quite frankly. God says it is "very good"—and so
should we.

Many years ago I taught a women's Bible class in a metropolitan city. Those who attended were clear-thinking,
sharp, "with it" ladies who genuinely desired to know their
Bibles and grow up spiritually. I'll never forget, however,
how many of them looked upon sex in their marriage as

● ● ●

something between a grim duty and a downright dirty experience! As I taught on marriage, I used this (and related passages) in Genesis. I recall how many were amazed to discover that marital sex was created by God in innocence and viewed by Him as "very good." One distraught and confused middle-aged woman saw me after the class and commented that she had always been convinced that "sex is part of the curse." Wrong!

Let's learn a lesson from Peter's experience in Acts 10. Let's realize that what God has cleansed we should no longer consider unholy. Now, I should add that sinful mankind has certainly twisted and polluted sex. There is every conceivable sexual perversion one can imagine, all of which are disgusting. But these are not to be confused with God's creation. Marital intimacy was, by His original design, to be enjoyed by married partners without guilt or without restraint. Note the way the Bible puts it in Hebrews 13:4.

> Let marriage be held in honor among all, and let the marriage bed be undefiled; for fornicators and adulterers God will judge.

This assures us that God views the marriage bed (another way of referring to marital intimacy) as "undefiled"—something He holds "in honor." You'll rekindle and preserve your marriage fire if you keep in mind that marital intimacy was created by God *prior to* the fall . . . and that He sees it as an undefiled, honorable part of your relationship with your mate.

*Intimacy: It Is for Pleasure*   There is a second biblical principle that will help keep your "honeymoon" from ending. Here is it:

• • •

*Intimacy in marriage was created for personal pleasure, not just for procreation.*

The fifth chapter of Proverbs is a picturesque chapter of warning. It shoots straight. Beginning on a negative note, Proverbs 5 talks first about defilement of the marriage relationship before it closes with a positive word about harmony and pleasure between husband and wife.

Listen first to the negative:

> My son, give attention to my wisdom,
>     Incline your ear to my understanding;
> That you may observe discretion,
>     And your lips may reserve knowledge.
> For the lips of an adulteress drip honey,
>     And smoother than oil is her speech;
> But in the end she is bitter as wormwood,
>     Sharp as a two-edged sword.
> Her feet go down to death,
>     Her steps lay hold of Sheol (vv. 1–5).

He goes on to describe the adulteress' feet as symbolic of the hellish life style she has adopted. If you go her way, he warns, you will wind up just like her. "Stay away!" shouts the man of wisdom.

But Solomon also adds some positive and encouraging words to his counsel. These words describe the refreshing harmony and physical pleasure God has designed for married partners to experience. The Living Bible says it well:

> Drink from your own well, my son—be faithful and true to your wife. Why should you beget children with women of the street? Why share your children with those outside your home? Let your manhood be a blessing; rejoice in the wife of your youth. Let her charms and

● ● ●

tender embrace satisfy you. Let her love alone fill you
with delight.

All right!

If you ever had the mistaken notion that God was some
sort of puritanical prude, this will certainly help dispel that
idea! No, He desires that our marriages provide us with
ecstatic sexual delights, exhilarating and pleasurable to the
maximum.

And in case you missed it, the passage veritably extols
intimate lovemaking, the joys of unrestrained, guilt-free
physical delight.

Not infrequently have I counseled with couples (especially wives) who entertain the mistaken idea that once the children are born, sex has served its purpose. You know, sort of
a "functional" mentality. How wrong! God's plan for intimacy between married partners is much broader than a bio-
logical necessity.

In another book by Solomon, we find similar words of
marital love. The wife in this passage is looking upon her
husband's body and is expressing her pleasure in his appearance.

> "My beloved one is tanned and handsome, better than
> ten thousand others! His head is purest gold, and he has
> wavy, raven hair. His eyes are like doves beside the water
> brooks, deep and quiet. His cheeks are like sweetly scent-
> ed beds of spices. His lips are perfumed lilies, his breath
> like myrrh. His arms are round bars of gold set with
> topaz; his body is bright ivory encrusted with jewels. His
> legs are as pillars of marble set in sockets of finest gold,
> like cedars of Lebanon; none can rival him."
>
> SONG OF SOLOMON 5:10–15, THE LIVING BIBLE

● ● ●

Wow! Wives, if you said that to your husband tonight, *no telling what could happen!*

And there's the other side of the coin as the husband views his wife:

> "How beautiful your tripping feet, O queenly maiden. Your rounded thighs are like jewels, the work of the most skilled of craftsmen. Your navel is lovely as a goblet filled with wine. Your waist is like a heap of wheat set about with lilies. Your two breasts are like two fawns, yes, lovely twins. Your neck is stately as an ivory tower, your eyes as limpid pools in Heshbon by the gate of Bath-rabbim. Your nose is shapely like the tower of Lebanon overlooking Damascus.
>
> "As Mount Carmel crowns the mountains, so your hair is your crown. The king is held captive in your queenly tresses.
>
> "Oh, how delightful you are; how pleasant, O love, for utter delight! You are tall and slim like a palm tree, and your breasts are like its clusters of dates. I said, I will climb up into the palm tree and take hold of its branches. Now may your breasts be like grape clusters, and the scent of your breath like apples, and your kisses as exciting as the best of wine, smooth and sweet, causing the lips of those who are asleep to speak."
>
> SONG OF SOLOMON 7:1–9, THE LIVING BIBLE

Now that man knew how to say it! We husbands can learn a lot from this. Our wives love to hear such things said so creatively. We would do well to cultivate the ability of verbalizing our admiration.

There can be no question about it, marital intimacy is for sheer pleasure, not just for enlarging the family.

• • •

*Intimacy: It Is Within Marriage*   A third principle about intimacy is written between the lines of 1 Corinthians 7:1–2. Let's read the verses before declaring the principle:

> Now concerning the things about which you wrote, it
> is good for a man not to touch a woman.
> But because of immoralities, let each man have his
> own wife, and let each woman have her own husband.

*Intimacy in marriage is planned for the husband-wife relationship only.*

Throughout Scripture, God makes it clear that intimacy is to be enjoyed by married partners. In our world of coed dorms, wife-swapping, swingers' clubs, and unisex, this principle sounds both irrelevant and stupid. But it is true. God designed us emotionally so that sex outside of marriage is not nearly as fulfilling or enjoyable as within that secure bond.

Tragic damages occur when God's standard is violated. Let me share just one for the sake of clarification.

A great deal of my counseling time is invested in the lives of couples planning to get married. During the three premarital counseling sessions, I probe deeply into their relationship. We discuss their lives from several perspectives: spiritually, emotionally, financially, socially, and sexually. It is not uncommon for those I plan to marry to have been intimately involved with each other. I require that this be stopped if such has been the case. Before we proceed I have each one promise me that from that day on (until they are married) they will sustain restraint and self-control in their relationship.

Here's why. If promiscuity is not completely stopped for a period of time before marriage, then after marriage a strange reversal in their roles occurs. The young bride marries with disappointment over the violation done against her by her fiancé. She soon becomes dominant and aggressive, taking

● ● ●

the role of leadership from her husband because of a mixture of resentment and anger. And the man? Well, he feels guilty, disappointed with himself, and ultimately becomes passive. She takes charge (and hates it) while he backs off (and feels miserable). All because their intimate relationship was incorrectly set in motion before marriage.

Of the hundreds of unhappy couples I have counseled who finally admitted to premarital promiscuity, I can hardly recall an exception to this strange pattern. A Christian psychologist friend of mine told me that the number one problem he deals with in his busy practice is the passive male.

So many men today find it difficult (impossible?) to take the proper role of authority in their home. I wonder how much of it stems from aggressive yet immoral, illicit involvements that were maintained during courtship days . . . and now they are suffering reverse consequences.

A number of years ago, a young man knocked very hard on the door of my study. I opened the door and found him weeping. It looked as though he either had a tragic accident or lost a close friend. I had never seen him before.

"My wife and I have had a terrible, terrible argument," he sobbed.

He looked very young, so I asked, "How long have you been married?"

"One month," he replied.

"Tell me what happened."

He told how he and his bride were involved in premarital intimacy for more than two years before their wedding.

"It had become a habitual part of our relationship, and it was fairly harmonious," he said. "We thought this would be the least of our problems when we married."

But within one month after their marriage, he and his new

• • •

bride experienced tremendous frustration to the point where she terribly resented his touching her. He even resented her role as she made advances toward him at times.

"As I talk with you about it," he said with sobs of remorse and sorrow, "I could not believe, even six months ago, that I could ever face a problem in this area. As a matter of fact, I'm impotent."

If you want your "honeymoon" not to end, start your marriage right. If you are already married, but you and your mate were heavily involved with each other, deal with that memory of compromise. Verbally, openly, humbly admit your guilt and seek each other's full forgiveness. God will honor such repentance.

***Intimacy: It Is Unselfish Affection*** The fourth principle, also in 1 Corinthians 7, is that *intimacy in marriage is an expression of unselfish affection, not selfish desire.*

> But because of immoralities, let each man have his own wife, and let each woman have her own husband.
> Let the husband fulfill his duty to his wife, and likewise also the wife to her husband (vv. 2–3).

What a tremendous difference it made in our marriage when I realized that intimacy in marriage was not simply for my own satisfaction, but for my *wife's* satisfaction. And from her point of view, it wasn't for her satisfaction, it was for *mine.* As Paul describes the "duty," he points out (v. 4) that the wife doesn't have authority over her own body. Clearly, he is referring to a lack of selfishness. She doesn't live with the selfish desire that she is going to be satisfied. She lives with that unselfish desire that her husband is going to be satisfied. Likewise, the husband doesn't have authority over his body, but the wife does. Both parties have a dual

● ● ●

role. They are to know pleasure and delight in fulfilling the desire of the other. It works both ways. It's a beautiful way to live.

Two illustrations may clarify this. First, consider the devoted, loving mother who faithfully prepares breakfast, lunch, and dinner for her family, day in and day out. Does she prepare all those meals to satisfy her own hunger? How often does she prepare a meal because the family is hungry? If your family is like ours, *often!* Her drive in carrying out the responsibilities of meal preparation is an unselfish drive that says, "I want to meet their needs." That's what the thought here is.

Or, think of the young man who has a tremendous future in business but decides that God has called him into the ministry. He enrolls in seminary for three or four more years (and takes on an internship) so that someday he might minister. He doesn't do that so that *he* might be satisfied. If he does, it really isn't God's calling at all. He does it so that needs in the lives of other people might be met. It isn't a selfish drive. If it's healthy, it's unselfish. That's how it's to be in marriage—an unselfish giving of oneself.

*Intimacy: It Is Uninterrupted*  The fifth principle is right here in verse 5: *Intimacy in marriage is not to be interrupted except on very rare occasions.*

> Stop depriving one another, except by agreement for a time that you may devote yourselves to prayer, and come together again lest Satan tempt you because of your lack of self-control.
>
> I Corinthians 7:5

This says that the healthy life and the healthy drive of a healthy husband and wife, however long they've been mar-

• • •

ried, is not to be restrained or squelched, except for three basic guidelines. First of all, by mutual agreement. Second, by a reason serious enough to call for prayer. Third, it should be temporary so that they might come together again.

I'm greatly concerned that this area is lacking in many Christian marriages. I have seen men and women who are tremendous Bible teachers and Bible students, but are feeble in this area of their lives. You may say, "Well, once the Lord takes first place, you really don't need such things as a strong sexual relationship."

God doesn't feel that way. Except on rare instances that drive shouldn't end. A sad witness to that is the great number of men in the ministry whose lives have gone down the moral tube.

## The Honeymoon: Why Can't It Begin . . . Again?

Why, though, does the honeymoon end? For some it may be much more complicated than I have described in this chapter. There may be a physical disability or mental disorder. That often calls for professional help. Others of you may be bogged down by ignorance. You are simply uninformed and use incorrect techniques. There are excellent, dependable books available today. Maybe you need to seek the counsel of someone who could wisely help you cultivate and develop this area. Two very excellent cassette tape albums for every married or soon-to-be married person who is searching for a medically accurate presentation of sex in marriage within the framework of the Bible's teaching are recorded by Ed Wheat, M.D., and Gaye Wheat of Springdale, Arkansas, and entitled "Intended for Pleasure" and "Love-Life." Their book, *Intended for Pleasure,* is published by Fleming H. Revell Company of Old Tappan, New Jersey.

● ● ●

Some may be victims of bad or tragic experiences. Perhaps you had a poor relationship with a father or mother. Maybe you were abused or raped. Those hurts must be healed if that is giving you difficulty.

Some may simply be bored, finding intimacy falling into a rut. They have become so set in a routine that the delights and ecstacies of marital love zoom out the window. If you believe in a honeymoon, then I'd suggest you now take a mini-moon. That's spelled M-I-N-I, but it could also be M-A-N-Y. Why not? Is your life so structured that you cannot get away for a weekend periodically without the books or briefcase or children? In our day, we need it. Look, if it was fun to walk on the beach when you were dating, it's fun now. Go do it!

I'm greatly concerned for missionaries who come back on furlough and pack their schedule back-to-back with meetings. They often need a honeymoon! In fact, they need it on the field. And wise are those couples who take time for it.

I find that the honeymoon sometimes ends simply because habits become set in concrete. For no special reason, couples just become disinterested and frigid. God planned intimacy to be warm, exciting, healthy, and growing. Break with the routine. Every once in a while, drop your wife a love note. (You might send a nitroglycerin tablet along with it so she can hold herself together when she gets it!) Pack a note in the suitcase when your husband takes a trip. Tell him what you think.

The other day we had a difficult morning at home. Everything broke loose. We couldn't get the kids to school on time and my wife was crying, the kids were crying, and I felt like crying because I was the cause of most of it. They all left and I was there alone. I sat down and wrote my wife a note:

• • •

Darling,

    I just want to thank you for all you mean to my life, for handling the numerous details that free me so I can do the things that I have to do. You'll never know what your life means to me. I admire you and I need you. I love you.

I thought she would look at it and think, "Hey, that's neat," toss it under the sink, and go right on. Do you know what she did? She taped it on the window in the front of the kitchen sink for all to read! My teenage son came home and spotted that note. As gushy as he could act it out, he read it *out loud.* That's the price you pay for being so romantic.

When did you last send your wife a note? When did you last give her flowers that weren't expected? When's the last time you surprised your loving mate with an expression of affection, wives? Or really caressed him and admitted your passion for him?

Singer Cliff Barrows of the Billy Graham team told me a few years ago about some of the ways he found to maintain delight and happiness in his own home. "I find marriages are held together by twelve words, Chuck," he said. "These are, 'I am wrong,' 'I am sorry,' 'Please forgive me,' and 'I love you.'"

"Hey, that's really good," I told him.

"Well," he replied, "they're not original with me. But I sure find that they work."

That was on Saturday night. On Sunday morning (the next day) I thought, "That would really be good in the sermon." So I shared them. Sunday night I thought, "This will really fit tonight's message." And so I used the list again. Wednesday night Bible study—I thought, "It's amazing how that list fits into this subject." So I rammed it in again. On

• • •

Saturday we had a wedding at the church. You guessed it. I used the list again in that ceremony.

A lady in our church had been in all four of those services. At the wedding reception she said to me, "Chuck, there are really sixteen words."

"Oh, really?" I said.

"Yes," she replied with a twinkle in her eye. "They are, 'I am wrong,' 'I am sorry,' 'Please forgive me,' 'I love you,' and *'This is a recording!'*"

She was right! You can say it like a recording or you can say it like you mean it.

My point in this long chapter is that if you are married and do not experience the delights of intimate love, you're missing the greatest privilege—intimately—that God provides on earth. And if you're missing it regularly, the honeymoon is over.

How about changing things?

How about starting today?

I dare you.

● ● ●

# 6

...

# Termites in Your Troth

...

I N THE 1960s I DEVELOPED a friendship with a very bright young student at Harvard. If you know anything about the school, you know they prefer only the top layer of the upper crust. He was in that category, intellectually, which always made me wonder why he liked to hang around me. I suppose the old saying is true: opposites attract.

In his intellectualism he had given up what he considered "unnecessary things," like haircuts, baths, deodorant, and toothpaste. But once you got past the smell, he was a terrific guy. Very genuine and sincere. Best of all, a warm heart for the Lord. Strange mixture, this fella. Crummy looking on the outside, but marvelous within. He always looked like he had just crawled out from under a bridge . . . but deep down inside, he was a winner.

...

Shortly after coming into a relationship with Jesus Christ, he kept other Christians on their toes—asking questions, probing the meaning of expressions and cliches so commonly used by the traditional troops. Some people got turned off. Frankly, I *loved* it! I really have him to thank for helping me forge out some of the finer points of communicating my theology—things I'd not thought through sufficiently. It was a healthy, meaningful relationship both ways.

He finally found a young woman with whom he fell in love . . . and before I knew it, they were discussing marriage. Their wedding turned out to be a real mismatch. Not the bride and groom; they fit each other perfectly. Still do. The difficulty was with the minister of the bride's church. He was supertraditional. This couple was supercasual, especially my unkempt friend, the groom. The minister preferred to use a ceremony that was straight from the book, sounding like it came out of either *King Lear* or William Bradford's files.

As the ceremony got under way, the "thees" and "thous" and "heretofores" and "whethersoevers" began to make my friend increasingly more nervous. But the worst part was that he couldn't interrupt and question what was going on. He frowned, fidgeted, looked up, sighed, bit his lip, wound his watch, scratched—the whole bit. I was having the time of my life watching him squirm!

Finally, the vows . . . the part where the preacher spoke and they were to follow the leader.

Dr. Drysdust came out with, "And unto thee I do pledge thee my troth."

That did it. Up till now, he had managed to maintain his composure (which was a minor miracle!), but no longer. The Harvard hotshot said, "I do pledge thee my *what?*"

Remember, this was right in the middle of the ceremony.

• • •

The pastor flinched (I was now smiling, I must confess) and cleared his throat as he repeated a little louder, "I do pledge thee my TROTH."

"What in the world is my *troth?*"

A conversation followed. It was the only ceremony I've ever heard done in dialogue! But it was also the most understandable part of all as the two men talked back and forth, discussing the meaning of words. I'll never forget that unique evening in New England.

It's because of that wedding I am particularly drawn to the archaic English term, "troth," in my chapter title.

It means "trust." A couple of centuries ago, it was commonly used for the "betrothal trust" between a couple getting married. The idea of a binding, solid commitment throughout time is in the word. As a bride and groom come to the altar, they promise to build their relationship on mutual trust. Or, at least, they *should*. And it is the trust that becomes the bond, humanly speaking, that cements the two together.

My concern is with the little things that gnaw away, weaken, and ultimately destroy a marriage. Like tiny termites in a house.

Since we're thinking about remodeling and restoring marriages in this volume, it's necessary that we address the subject of termites that get into our "troth."

## Small Things, Not Big

I'm convinced it's not the big things that weaken a marriage. On the contrary, big problems frequently *strengthen* marriages. The loss of a job, sudden illness, the death of a child, long absences because of military service—these more often than not deepen our love and enhance a relationship.

• • •

It's the little things. The slow leaks, not the blowouts. The insidious "pests" we seldom even consider that cut away at the heart of a home until finally, it crumbles as two people walk away.

## Needed: An Inspection Report

Turn again to the Song of Solomon, the book we blushed our way through in the previous chapter. In the picturesque language of a lover, the husband is speaking to his wife. It's an intimate scene (most of them are in this book!), one of deep affection, tender and romantic. Listen.

> "O my dove, in the clefts of the rock,
> In the secret place of the steep pathway,
> Let me see your form,
> Let me hear your voice;
> For your voice is sweet,
> And your form is lovely" (2:14).

But then, out of the blue, he declares a warning, a word of caution . . .

> "Catch the foxes for us,
> The little foxes that are ruining the vineyards,
> While our vineyards are in blossom" (2:15).

It's like a cymbal crash in a lullaby. The man, however, is concerned that their "vineyard" (growing, delightful relationship) not be destroyed by "foxes" (those little "termites" that eat away at a relationship). So naturally, like an inspector, he sends out a warning signal. "Catch the foxes!" Or, in light of our analogy, "Kill the pests!" Implied here is the very real fact that pests are always present, always ready to devour the blossoms. The couple that forgets that fact is ripe and ready for an invasion into their vineyard.

• • •

You may be surprised to know that more structures are destroyed by termites than by fire each year. Incredible as it may seem, these tiny, silent, industrious insects create greater havoc than the lashing, brutal, headline-making flames of fire.

## Four "Termites" That Weaken Marriages

Turn now to the fifth chapter of Ephesians. The last thirteen verses of this grand chapter are perhaps the most familiar words in all the New Testament on marriage. Everything in the chapter builds like a climax to those verses. But I'd like us to back up to verses 15–21, the paragraph just before the finale. It is here we shall find four of the more common termites that weaken the marriage bond.

First, however, read these verses slowly, preferably aloud:

> Therefore be careful how you walk, not as unwise men, but as wise, making the most of your time, because the days are evil. So then do not be foolish, but understand what the will of the Lord is. And do not get drunk with wine, for that is dissipation, but be filled with the Spirit, speaking to one another in psalms and hymns and spiritual songs, singing and making melody with your heart to the Lord; always giving thanks for all things in the name of our Lord Jesus Christ to God, even the Father; and be subject to one another in the fear of Christ.
>
> EPHESIANS 5:15–21

*Confusion*   Go back to verse 15 and read it one more time. Paul begins with an imperative, a strong command. "Be careful!" The New International Version says, "Be very careful!" Literally, the Greek terms convey the thought of con-

•  •  •

tinuing to take heed how accurately, how exactly you conduct yourself. Here's the idea: "Keep on taking heed how accurately you are conducting your life!" He is pleading for some honest self-analysis. Painful, but needed.

Since we are thinking about marriage, "Keep on taking heed how accurately you fulfill your role as a husband or wife!" In order to accomplish this, you need a ruler, a standard. Without that, you are in a continual state of confusion. Uncertainty abounds. The standard, of course, is your Bible: the reliable, inerrant guide to direct your thought correctly. By turning to this Book you gain a proper perspective, a guideline to follow. The termite of confusion is forced out of your relationship as you gain a clear understanding of your responsibility.

I have observed three major reasons why husbands and wives get confused about their roles in marriage.

First, they are assaulted by the secular propaganda opposed to a monogamous relationship. You listen long enough to garbage like "Marriage is obsolete!" and "Swingers have more fun" and "It's degrading for a woman to be in submission to any man" . . . and before long, you develop what the experts are calling "floating anxieties." That's a four-bit expression for "confusion."

Second, confusion often increases because of the complexity of interpersonal relationships. Let me explain. A husband and a wife enjoy a simple, uncomplicated, one-on-one relationship. This basic interpersonal relationship is relatively easy to maintain—until a child comes on the scene. Suddenly, it jumps to three: husband-wife . . . momma-baby . . . daddy-baby. When *another* child arrives, there are now six interpersonal relationships. If you have four children (as we do), hang on. It jumps to 15. Five children? You have 21

• • •

interpersonal relationships bouncing around your pad. You get any more and you'll need to computerize the thing! And how does this add to the confusion? Well, a wife and mother starts asking, "Am I a cook . . . laundry woman . . . chauffeur . . . seamstress? Or mistress . . . partner . . . counselor . . . traveling companion? Or P.T.A. officer . . . financier . . . student . . . Ms. Everything?" Confusion also assaults dad who is beginning his mid-life crisis to boot.

Third, some couples are just plain immature. How many of us have to admit we grew up *after* we got married? I know I did. So did Cynthia. We dated one week before I asked her to marry me. That's right, friends and neighbors, I waited that long so I'd be sure I had the right one. She was 16, I was 18. Really mature, really stable. We married 18 months later. Our children tease their mom by telling others I had to sign her report card. That isn't true. We certainly waited until she got out of high school before we got married. Two weeks. We had the maturity of a couple of nanny goats—and more stubbornness than a whole pen full of 'em.

In 25 years, we've worked through a lot of confusion. And I'll tell you, without a Bible to keep us on course, no way! Take away the Scriptures and I wouldn't predict two years of harmony for any couple . . . for some, not even two months. The confusion termite is a killer. Only God's truth can exterminate it.

*Too Busy*  There is another home-wrecker—the too-busy termite. Read Ephesians 5:15–16 again.

> Therefore be careful how you walk, not as unwise
> men, but as wise, making the most of your time, because
> the days are evil.

• • •

Something that is evil is in direct opposition to the good. That describes the day in which we live. Evil. Designed to oppose what is good. Many a couple is caught in the trap of becoming too busy. Not necessarily bad things, just too *many* things.

What a strange species we are! Man is the only animal that runs faster when he loses his way. The result? Increased irritability. Frayed nerves. Impatience. Shorter fuse. Preoccupation. Procrastination when it comes to choosing the right priorities. Yes, such days are "evil." Don't dodge it, face it. Admit it.

Better than that, let's adopt the scriptural injunction and start "making the most of your time."

In *The Family First* (good title), the author, Kenneth Gangel, writes convicting words.

> The man who must travel one hour each way to his business in the city besides spending eight or nine hours there, finds himself on the short end of the clock when it becomes necessary to spend some time with wife and children. But here again we are dealing with the matter of priorities. It is not so much a question of how the husband spends all his time, but rather how he chooses to spend that time which he can afford to invest as he chooses.[1]

That's the kind of thing husbands and wives *must* address. And it's been my observation that Christian couples are the worst offenders. For some reason we are beginning to crank out more workaholics, more high-achieving neurotics, more nervous, anxiety-prone people than ever before. Many a child watches with bewilderment as Mom and Dad ricochet from room to room in the house, speed to one meeting after

• • •

another, cram down Big Macs, often dumping out religious cliches en route. Who are we kidding? Being too busy is not a friend, it's an enemy to a home. An evil, selfish, demanding force that requires things of us, things we have no business surrendering.

A designer friend of mine, Paul Lewis, recently introduced me to an outstanding little book. I sat down and read it in one sitting. It's called *When I Relax I Feel Guilty*. Buy it. Read it. Even if you have to cancel a meeting. Your health deserves it. So does your marriage.

In this fine book by Tim Hansel, a poem by Orin L. Crain appears that is really worth your time. I share it with you, but I would add, don't hurry through it. Digest it. Read it—perhaps twice.

## SLOW ME DOWN, LORD[2]

Slow me down, Lord.

Ease the pounding of my heart by the quieting of my mind.

Steady my hurried pace with a vision of the eternal reach of time.

Give me, amid the confusion of the day, the calmness of the everlasting hills.

Break the tensions of my nerves and muscles with the soothing music of the singing streams that live in my memory.

Teach me the art of taking minute vacations—of slowing down to look at a flower, to chat with a friend, to pat a dog, to smile at a child, to read a few lines from a good book.

● ● ●

Slow me down, Lord, and inspire me to send my roots deep into the soil of life's enduring values, that I may grow toward my greater destiny.

Remind me each day that the race is not always to the swift; that there is more to life than increasing its speed.

Let me look upward to the towering oak and know that it grew great and strong because it grew slowly and well.

ORIN L. CRAIN

Isn't that penetrating? Believe me, the too-busy termite will ultimately ruin your marriage if you let it remain in your home. It will turn you into a fanatical, determined, stern race horse that is unable (ultimately) to slow down. A prime subject for a coronary. Let me say it directly, pulling no punches. No amount of fanatical zeal or noble calling will ever justify the destruction of a home . . . I don't care how religious the reason or how spiritual the squirrel cage!

Hear the testimony of a former workaholic, get rid of that too-busy termite, *or else.*

*Insensitivity* We've considered the confused termite and the too-busy termite. Both are disastrous to a marriage. There's another—the dull termite. Look again at Ephesians 5:17:

So then do not be foolish, but understand what the will of the Lord is.

Centuries before Paul originally wrote these words, the Hebrews had a term for "fool." It was from a verb that meant "dull, insensitive." Like a thick callus impervious to feeling.

The same idea is carried out here in the Ephesian letter. Literally, it's a present imperative, a command, suggesting

• • •

either "Stop being thick . . . !" or "Don't get into the habit of being thick!" Applying it to a marriage, as we are doing, God is saying, "Quit being so insensitive and inconsiderate of your mate!" Good, wise, needed counsel.

When the dull termite invades a marriage (it usually takes this species a few years), it prompts thinking like, "I'm really not aware of what's happening," or worse, "I really don't care much anymore . . . it's not worth the effort." God says strongly, "Stop thinking like that! Quit it! Break that habit!"

But how?

How can a couple get rid of a dull, insensitive spirit between them? Well, look back at the seventeenth verse. God places a positive immediately after the negative command. The two complement each other.

> ". . . but understand what the will of the Lord is."

The key to this is "understanding." An old, reliable, New Testament authority states the problem of insensitivity:

> ". . . the lack of common-sense perception of the reality of things."[3]

God offers a solution—think keenly, using common sense, about what the will of the Lord is for you as a wife, as a husband. Breaking the thick, insensitive barrier in a marriage is tough, but not impossible.

Most every summer the Swindoll family enjoys a week or so at Mount Hermon, a lovely, picturesque, Christian conference grounds nestled in the cool, wooded hillside along the coast near Santa Cruz. Some of our most treasured memories are related to the days we have spent in that delightful setting. A couple of years ago I spoke at a family conference there, and we became acquainted with a family that had

•  •  •

come for their first time. The dad was a bright, ⸢
and-coming young executive with an aggressiv⸢
West Coast. His wife was equally intelligent, a⸢
a loving mother of their three children. I spoke
the family, drawing various principles out of t⸢
explaining how relevant they were for today. I
time. As always, God's Word did the job
changed.

As the week began to unfold, I started taking
est in this couple. They reminded me of two ⸢
birds. Each time we gathered for another sessio⸢
were, loving every minute of it, gulping down
insight after another.

Before we left on Saturday they came ove⸢
embraced me, both of them sobbing audibly. In ⸢
od of time they spilled out their story. Throug⸢
admitted they had fallen into this subtle trap of i⸢
He was preoccupied with his work, climbing th⸢
ladder, and determined to get to the top before h⸢
years of age. She, in turn, compensated by bein⸢
mom, trying to replace the absent father and pr⸢
the things her kids needed. Both were spinning ⸢
orbits, hardly aware of the other's goals and conc⸢

No extramarital affairs. No huge, lengthy argu⸢
even a thought of divorce. But separate lives. Like the song,
they modeled these words:

> "Two different worlds we live in. . . ."

Their growing insensitivity was exposed as they turned to
the Scriptures and listened to its counsel on the home. They
literally "understood what the will of the Lord is" and they
*both* submitted themselves to it. An internal revolution

● ● ●

occurred that week in that marriage. For the first time in years they began to listen to and care for and be aware of each other. To use Paul's words, they "stopped being foolish." The dull termite was exterminated in that couple's marriage at Mount Hermon that summer.

Before closing the chapter, there is one more devastating termite that weakens a marriage troth. As soon as I name it, you'll agree.

*Stubbornness* Yes, just plain bull-headedness. The stubborn termite can make a home a hell.

Ephesians 5:18–21 says:

> And do not get drunk with wine, for that is dissipation, but be filled with the Spirit,
> speaking to one another in psalms and hymns and spiritual songs, singing and making melody with your heart to the Lord;
> always giving thanks for all things in the name of our Lord Jesus Christ to God, even the Father;
> and be subject to one another in the fear of Christ.

There's a lot of interesting and important theology here, but let's try to stick with the subject of marriage since that's what the passage is leading to in verses 22–33.

Highlight in your mind the last verse, verse 21. It says, ". . . be subject to one another. . . ." Are you ready for that? *Mutual* submission is rarely mentioned. The New International Version renders this:

> Submit to one another out of reverence for Christ.

That's the secret! The only way the stubborn termite can be exterminated is through an all-out respect for Christ. Eyes

• • •

on Him. A deep, genuine, wholesome reverence for Christ Jesus as Lord.

Stubborn feelings can be subtle, almost hidden. "I can't stand it, but I will grit my teeth and bear it. I will live with you, but don't expect me to cooperate." And on the other hand a stubborn will can be very obvious and obnoxious. "No way am I going to give in! This is what I want and it's what I'm gonna get!" I say a lot about martial fights in the next chapter, but suffice it to say here, this stubborn resistance creates more arguments and conflicts than any other single problem in marriage. The stubborn termite, as it begins to do its damage, turns holy wedlock into an unholy deadlock. Incompatibility and anger replace harmony and peace. Misery moves in. In spades.

Why? Back to verse 21. Because of an unwillingness on the part of either or both partners to surrender . . . to do precisely as God has declared.

## Operation Extermination

If you're serious about your "troth" and you really want to reaffirm your vows before God, four termites must be exterminated.

1. Confusion
2. Too busy
3. Insensitivity
4. Stubborness

Here's how. With God's help, you can locate and exterminate. But it will require two-fisted determination.

First, *openly admit the termites have invaded.* Quit denying the truth. As the light of the Word of God has shined brightly, bringing the real facts out of hiding, say so. Deny it no longer. Identify the pest(s) by name. In doing so, admit

● ● ●

your culpability, your struggle, your tendency toward that particular problem.

From fourth grade until I entered seminary, my home was in Houston. You know Houston—humidity city! Wall-to-wall bugs. It's unreal. Even though my spotlessly clean mother denied it, our home had roaches. To her, our place was off-limits to those nasty creatures . . . but they apparently didn't get the message. I finally decided to prove to her they were really there. We quietly tiptoed to the kitchen door one night. I snapped on the light and she screamed. Those guys must have been having a rodeo between the range and the refrigerator. Startled, they scattered in all four directions as mother covered her eyes. The light exposed them. From then on she admitted the problem. We had roaches!

Maybe you're a positive-thinking kind of marriage partner. That's okay, just so you're not denying reality. If termites are in your troth, say so! If the light of Scripture has exposed them, the first step toward correction is admission.

Second, *discuss and then determine how you plan to control them.* Being aware of termites then doing nothing about them is ridiculous. Since they are the only insect that never sleeps (even the pest world has workaholics), they stay at the task incessantly. They *must* be controlled. So must the bothersome, irritating, destructive pests in your marriage. Like termites, you may not be able to get rid of them all permanently, but you can certainly exterminate enough to guarantee salvaging your home. Be up front with your partner. Seek some solutions.

Third, *start today.* Not tomorrow. Not when you finish this book . . . or when you make promises to cooperate. No, *now.* Today. Ask your Lord to deal directly with your part of the problem. Please . . . do not put it off.

• • •

Remember when you "pledged your troth?" God heard your promise. He smiles on every effort you make to keep that promise . . . to strengthen your trust.

Is He still smiling?

## Notes

1. Dr. Kenneth Gangel, *The Family First* (Winona Lake, Indiana: BMH Books, 1972), p. 116.

2. Tim Hansel, *When I Relax I Feel Guilty* (Elgin, Illinois: David C. Cook Publishing Co., 1979), p. 9.

3. W. E. Vine, *An Expository Dictionary of New Testament Words,* 4 vols. (Old Tappan, New Jersey: Fleming H. Revell Company, 1940), 2:113.

● ● ●

# 7
. . .

# How to Have a Good Fight

OU WILL BE SURPRISED to know I grew up in a home next door to a boxing ring. That's right, ringside every Saturday night. Preliminary bouts were held during week nights, but the main event was always on Saturday night. Late. Like somewhere between 11:30 and 1:00 in the morning.

The fights were never fair. There was an 11-year-old bantam weight, a welter-weight dad, and (I'll be gracious) a light-heavy-weight mom. What a scene!

When the main event began, the three Swindoll kids would quickly gather in the boys' room, turn off the light, push open the window, and watch it happen. My mother would put on the popcorn and serve it up with cokes or hot chocolate. I'll tell you, it was better than Hawaii Five-O, Kojak, the Rockford Files, and the Dukes of Hazzard all

. . .

wrapped up into one. It was the best show in East Houston—always unpredictable and exciting. Frankly, I was sorry to see those folks finally move.

Two things stick in my mind when I remember those people next door. First, they owned a radio which served as the ring bell, the gong. When it came flying out onto their screened-in porch, we knew the fight was almost over. Second, they drove a 1941 *Lincoln Zephyr*—a huge, 16-cylinder set of wheels that had no muffler—which always announced their arrival. Soon as we'd hear the screech of the tires and the Sherman-tank roar of their Lincoln, we'd pile up on the bed and stare in childlike wonder.

It began in the driveway around the car with five or ten minutes of chasing. Then one got inside and the lights snapped on. Of course, they had no shades to draw and there were no rules and no bells. It was just hand-to-hand combat from start to finish. It lasted anywhere from ten minutes to one night's record of two hours.

I'll never forget those Saturday nights. After we were sent to bed, I'd lie awake wondering how many families in that vast metropolis were fighting that night.

### Fights Are Common

As I grew up, I became friends with a fellow who drove an emergency vehicle for the Mercy Corps, a paramedics organization. At times he took me along and I discovered a lot of other houses were also boxing rings inside.

Even now, I am amazed how often I come across people who fight. Occasionally, the highly educated fight. Even Christians fight. I don't mean people will always fight with their fists, but sometimes that happens, too. A while ago, a born-again Christian man told me that he had great difficul-

• • •

ty restraining his anger. It was not uncommon for him to strike his wife and children several times. He was deeply concerned about what prompted that behavior.

If the truth were known, not some, but *most* marriages are marked by periodic skirmishes—occasionally an all-out *war*. Frequently, the marital warfare is in the trenches of belligerence or moodiness. Some battles are "night attacks" or surprise assaults. Others are cold wars of stoic silence. Cruel methods of torture are also employed—public criticism, fearful threats, intimidation, ugly sarcasm, and hateful remarks designed to put down one's mate.

Such tactics are popular . . . but *wrong* because they are unfair and they never lead to domestic peace. It may be impossible to stamp out fighting completely, but in this chapter we want to learn why couples fight, and then what rules can keep it clean, good, and beneficial.

## Why Do Couples Fight?

From my years of witnessing fights and the results of those fights in counseling, I've come up with two basic facts about fights. First, most couples don't fight until after they marry. Seldom do you find an engaged couple fighting with each other. Why do things change when people marry? Everything before you say "I do" is voluntary, but after you say "I do," it's compulsory. Right? Beforehand, there is an open end, but afterwards you are boxed in (no pun intended). Furthermore, when people go together, they usually aren't totally honest. They put their best foot forward and act as though they like things they don't.

For example, the girl loves opera and the guy hates it. She sighs, "Oh, I'd love to go see 'Carmen.'" He lies, "Oh, I'd *love* to go, too!" What does he do? He buys two tickets and

• • •

takes her to "Carmen." He hates every warble of it, but he doesn't say so. After they marry, she says, "Honey, let's go to the opera." He says, "I hate opera!" She doesn't understand why, and if the truth were known, he doesn't understand why he lied before they were married. But he did.

Or, the girl hates fishing, but the guy loves it. Before they're married, he says, "I'll come by and pick you up at 3:30 in the morning and we'll zing down to the lake and fish all day." She gushes (deceitfully), "Wonderful!" So she gets up at 2:30 in the morning, thoughtfully packs a lunch, and piles in the car promptly at 3:30. She's singing and telling him how much she loves him, and they fish all day. Then they get married. Several months later he says, "Honey, let's get up and go fishing." She says, "Not me. I can't stand fishing."

"Why? You used to go."

GONG! The fight starts.

And it even goes deeper. Before the marriage the fellow initiates the love relationship. He's assertive and decisive. She loves it. After marriage he looks upon his bride as someone to take care of him. She is still expecting the role of leadership to flow, but it doesn't. See the problem—why couples often fight not before, but after marriage?

There's another fact we dare not overlook: Most fights are not fair, so no one wins and both lose! In these fights, couples resort to unbiblical, dirty tactics . . . to physical and verbal abuse, slamming one another to the mat with ugly, rejecting statements.

Disagreements are part of marriage. We have to be realistic. Two strong, independent people will not flow together without some turbulence.

Several years ago I visited Pittsburgh and stayed in a hotel

● ● ●

that overlooked the confluence of two rivers—the Allegheny and Monongahela. Where those two massive rivers become one larger river, the mighty Ohio River, the current is very strong.

That's how it is in a marriage. When two strong, independent persons flow together at the altar, a lot of power is generated. Suddenly, in some cases, a virtual hell breaks loose and the couple wonders what's wrong. But it is a natural problem that has to be worked through. Fights occur. Few are the couples who can honestly say they've never fought.

## Rules On How To Keep It Clean

How can couples flow together in the current and still stay together in harmony? Ephesians 4:25–32 will be the guide to answering this. It offers *seven rules* for having a good fight. These rules will allow you to carry on normal, natural, disagreeable times without breaking with Scripture. If you are the fighting type, I'd urge you to write down the rules and even put them in a prominent place so you can refer to them until they become a part of your life. The scriptural basis:

> Therefore, laying aside falsehood, speak truth, each one of you, with his neighbor, for we are members of one another.
> Be angry, and yet do not sin; do not let the sun go down on your anger,
> and do not give the devil an opportunity.
> Let him who steals steal no longer; but rather let him labor, performing with his own hands what is good, in order that he may have something to share with him who has need.
> Let no unwholesome word proceed from your mouth, but only such a word as is good for edification according

● ● ●

to the need of the moment, that it may give grace to those who hear.

And do not grieve the Holy Spirit of God, by whom you were sealed for the day of redemption.

Let all bitterness and wrath and anger and clamor and slander be put away from you, along with all malice.

And be kind to one another, tender-hearted, forgiving each other, just as God in Christ also has forgiven you.

EPHESIANS 4:25–32

***Keep It Honest***  Rule one is from verse 25: *Be committed to honesty and mutual respect.* If you were to read that twenty-fifth verse as Paul wrote it, it would read: "Therefore, having laid aside falsehood, talk truth." In Greek there is a particular verb tense that conveys the idea of something being done in a point of time. There is a different verb tense to convey the idea of continued action, going on day after day. The particular verb here for "laying aside" is the former, rather than the latter. And when it appears in the sentence with a main verb, it always precedes the action of the main verb. In other words, the laying aside is to be done in a point of time . . . and ahead of the fact that you will now start telling the truth. That's why I rendered it, "Therefore, *having* laid aside lying, talk truthfully."

I'm calling this a commitment because of the thought here of having already done something. This isn't something that you do day after day after day. Rather, as a husband to a wife and a wife to a husband, you commit yourself by saying, "Honey, no matter what, I want you to know that from this point and forever in our relationship, it is my deep desire to be honest with you and to respect you as a person." It is not something that is repeated in a half-hearted way time and time again throughout a marriage.

• • •

Some of you have never made that commitment. At the altar you vowed certain things. But have you ever committed yourself, verbally and honestly in your soul, to being authentic and honest with your partner, viewing your partner with respect? I get the idea of showing respect from the last part of verse 25: "Speak truth, each one of you, with his neighbor, for we are members of one another."

I perform weddings only for people who are born-again—only for Christians. That's because I believe that when you marry another born-again person, you take on not only a wife or husband but also a brother or sister in the faith. You're not just marrying a man or woman; you are marrying another member of the family of God. That adds an essential dimension to your marriage. Just as you would hold in high respect someone sitting in your pew, you would also do the same for your marriage partner. That's why I'm suggesting that there be a commitment of this kind.

It is essential that you commit yourself to an honest relationship, ideally even before you marry, so that you do not fall into the trap of acting, of lying to each other just to win your partner over. I am deeply concerned that couples who date start off right from the beginning with total honesty. They need to say, "Let's not try to kid each other. Let's not play games, I want to be honest with you and I want you to be honest with me. I can take it and I will give it back with tact." Then when fights occur, no one is set up for a surprise punch.

*Keep It Under Control*   After being committed to honesty and mutual respect, the second rule is: *Make sure your weapons are not deadly.*

> Be angry, and yet do not sin (v. 26).

• • •

Maybe you have never really understood this verse. Scholars commonly call it a permissive imperative. That means that God is not commanding you to blow your stack. God is permitting you to be angry on certain occasions, but He is warning you not to let it lead to sin, because sin leads to a death-like existence. That's why the weapons of anger can be deadly.

I find a green light in this verse for anger. He says, "I permit you to be angry, but I say to you (with the same stroke of the pen before the ink is dry), don't let that anger lead to sin." All of us know in our consciences when anger has become sin. I don't have to spell that out for you. Bursts of temper are sinful. Anger that slips out of control is sinful. Anger that plans to hurt another member of the family or another individual is sinful anger. Anger that is expressed in profanity is, too. You know the point where your anger becomes sin. That's the point he has in mind.

Proverbs 18:14 tells us why it's important not to have deadly weapons and not to employ deadly words:

> The spirit of a man can endure his sickness, but a broken spirit who can bear?

I want you to remember the last part of this contrastive proverb. A man or woman can endure sickness, but they cannot endure a broken spirit. In other places in Proverbs, this is called a crushed spirit. The crushing of the spirit of a child is different from the breaking of the child's self-will. You don't want to do the crushing, but you want to do the breaking. The same is true in a marriage relationship. Verse 19 of the same chapter in Proverbs shows why it's important:

● ● ●

A brother offended [*a wife offended, a husband offended*] is harder to be won than a strong city, and contentions are like the bars of a castle [*brackets are mine*].

Have you ever been wounded or crushed by your mate? I'm sure that we all have at times. Angry words said in the spur of the moment are deadly weapons. When we attack the person rather than the problem, we move into deadly areas. When we make things personal or assault motives rather than dealing with the wrong *situation,* we're treading on thin ice. When we reject rather than reprove, it's harmful.

One man bitterly told me that his father-in-law once announced, "I never did have much use for you after all!" He will never forget that statement until the day of his death. Never. That man used a deadly weapon on his son-in-law. So did the mate who cracked, "No wonder you have a brother in the mental hospital." Or, "I can't stand the way you look." Or, "Those freckles, they're terrible!" Or, "Let's face it, you're ugly, just plain ugly." In a moment of anger, you may actually say that kind of thing, but it's deadly! Your mate may later say, "I forgive you. That's all right. I understand." But deep inside, it's doubtful that will ever be fully forgotten. It's crushing. It breaks that inner spirit that is so much a part of a marriage. Make sure your weapons don't lead to sin. Lay down your deadly arms.

Before coming to the next rule, let me caution you against gross exaggeration. Try to remember to remove the words "always" and "never" from your fights. They have no place because those sweeping universal rebukes are not true. No one "always" or "never" does something. There is an exception somewhere.

• • •

***Keep It Timed Right*** The third rule: *Agree together that the time is right.* This comes after you've committed yourself to honesty and mutual respect and thrown away the deadly weapons so you're now under control. Look at verses 26–27:

> Do not let the sun go down on your anger, and do not
> give the devil an opportunity.

That's very wise counsel. Paul is not only being specific about not letting anger build up day after day, night after night, but he is implying here the wise use of time. He is suggesting that there is a time in which arguments are to take place. There is the proper time to disagree and there is the proper time *not* to disagree.

Perhaps the most important word in this rule is "together." Be sure that both of you sense that this is the right time to talk. And that's not when husbands come in from work and battle fatigue has set in over his day. Not when wives face a mound of dishes. Or either is fatigued. There are certain times we are not ready to talk in-depth about serious and disagreeable things. Wise are the husbands and wives who know the timing. And if you have that first rule down, you will be honest enough to say, "Honey, this isn't the best time" or "Let's talk a little later when the children are down," or "This isn't the right place to do it. Let's deal with it a little later." And when you say that, keep your appointment. Set the time and don't put it off.

Frequently, couples have battle flags that they wave when they're in need of talking. Mates who are sensitive (last chapter, remember?) learn to read the signals. A husband may become very quiet. A wife may talk rapidly on the phone to her husband and hang up almost before he's

● ● ●

through. The husband may show he can't handle more irritation by swearing at the traffic. Your mate may not eat. Or, he bites his fingernails. Get to know those battle flags. Don't let them pass unheeded. Bring the subject up rather calmly. Say, "Could we talk right now, or before long? I'd like us to do it when the time is right." Plan your timing together.

*Keep It Positive*   Rule four (this is one of my favorites): *Be ready with a positive solution right after taking a swing.* I get this from verse 28. Although Paul is dealing here with the problem of stealing, let's apply the principle to marriage. He makes a statement and then takes a strong swing at it: "Let him who steals, steal no longer." No doubt where he stands on the issue. "I don't want that to go on any longer," he says. "It's wrong before God. There's no way you can justify it. Don't steal." But, he comes right back with a positive, supportive solution:

> Rather let him labor, performing with his own hands what is good, in order that he may have something to share with him who has need.

After taking a swing at the problem of stealing, he suggests a healthy, workable alternative: "I'm not going to leave you dangling, telling thieves not to steal. That alone doesn't do any good. I'm going to tell you how you can help it." An elder in a former church used to say, "I won't listen to any criticism in this church if a person doesn't offer, along with the criticism, a suggestion on how we might correct the problem." Not a bad idea! When you come to your mate with justified criticism, be quick with a suggested solution. Criticism hurts. A positive, supportive comment will help take some of the sting out of the wound.

• • •

This is where I have often been weak in my own marriage. My wife's been with the kids 12 to 14 hours during the day, and I walk in and say, "You're very irritated, aren't you?" That's really a wonderful way to begin an evening with the wife! Or, "Don't get so discouraged. You'll be through with the dishes by eleven o'clock." I soon began to realize that such comments don't do anything but drive the hurt deeper. How much better to say, "Sweetheart, you must be exhausted. Let me work with you in this." Or, "Honey, I've discovered that when I get irritated with our children, this helps."

Coming back with a positive solution helps support the person who is already demoralized in his spirit. Paul is not only telling the thief that it is wrong to steal, he also tells him what to do about it. He says, "Go to work so that you learn the joys of giving, and then you'll not want to steal." Remember: Condemnation without hope crushes.

**Keep It Tactful**   Rule five: *Watch your words and guard your tone.* In brief, use tact. This probably will be the most difficult rule to implement because when we have a point to make that we feel very strongly about, we tend to get louder. When we get softer, though, we say more. The louder our voices, the less our mate will hear; the uglier the words, the less we will communicate. Paul says in verse 29:

> Let no unwholesome word proceed from your mouth. . . .

"Unwholesome" means "rotten, putrid." It certainly would include profanity and swearing, bitter words. But look at how gracious Paul is. He doesn't just attack. He says, in effect, here's the other side:

• • •

. . . but only such a word as is good for edification according to the need of the moment, that it may give grace to those who hear.

You can cultivate such an honest and mutually respected relationship with your mate that both of you can live with a teachable spirit toward one another. But the bond is tactfulness. In his book *Family Communication,* Sven Wahlroos has written one of the finest pieces on tact I've ever read. Here's part of it:

> . . . tactfulness is an approach to another human being which involves being sincere and open in communication while at the same time showing respect for the other person's feelings and taking care not to hurt him unnecessarily. Tactfulness involves an implicit trust or faith in the other person and communicates the message: "I trust that you will be able to handle what I'm going to tell you, as long as I respect your feelings and do my best to guard against my own destructive tendencies so that I don't hurt you unnecessarily."[1]

This is profound. With tact, you say, "I trust you and I trust as I share these words I won't hurt you unnecessarily." Unless it's a very unusual situation or your wife or husband is a very unusual person, that will absolutely disarm them if it's said in sincerity.

I have found that our home has its most productive "fights" when that kind of groundwork was laid. We need to say, "Look, honey, I don't personally agree with you right now. I know you don't agree with me, either, but whatever we say from this point on, let's understand, we don't want to hurt the other. We want to come to the right conclusion." And then we get into it. Tact does wonders when it comes to removing a defensive spirit.

•  •  •

Verse 30 says, "Do not grieve the Holy Spirit of God." You understand that when you do sin, whether it's at home in your heart, or in public, you have grieved the Spirit. He says, "Let's not do that."

*Keep It Private*   The sixth rule for a good fight is: *Don't swing at your mate in public.* That's from verse 31:

> Let all bitterness and wrath and anger and clamor and slander be put away from you, along with all malice.

When you swing in public, your malice is showing. There are at least two ways that you can do this in a marriage. First of all, you can do it with open, bold embarrassment. Second, you can do it with subtle, cutting sarcasm. Either one hurts deeply.

In a church I formerly served many years ago, a husband was having a great deal of difficulty with his strong-willed wife. As a result, he became increasingly strong-willed as well (this often happens), and their home became a volatile powder keg. One Sunday morning in which I had spoken on living the Christian life at home, he just threw up his arms in despair. He was crushed in his own spirit before God. He was hurt, realizing that he had been wrong to use the same aggressive tactics.

He came to me in the vestibule of the church, which was jammed with probably 50 people. Some were involved in conversations, some were trying to get out, and others were browsing through some literature. He began to share privately the overflow of his hurt, and very quietly admitted to me, "I have caused havoc in our home this week. I confess in my rage I swore at her the other day. I'm embarrassed to

• • •

admit our home is a wreck. Why, just last Tuesday, I was ready to walk. . . ."

About that time his wife came up. She hadn't heard his confession, his contrite spirit, only the last part where he said, "Our home is a wreck." With a fair amount of volume, she said, "It's because of your *black heart* that our home is a wreck!" The vestibule hushed. As he reddened, she maliciously sliced away at him for everyone to hear. He was devastated. I was embarrassed for him . . . and others blushed and walked away.

You never take your dirty laundry to church to wash it out, do you? Nor do you bring it along to social gatherings, do you? No, you put it where it belongs. You deal with it there. That's where your dirty laundry from a relationship ought to stay. Except in cases of personal counsel with a trusted confidant, don't share the soiled details of your marriage in public. That only succeeds in amassing a group of people who pity you and your terrible plight. Or it embarrasses them. Down in your soul, you know that if your husband or your wife were ever to hear the problems publicly proclaimed, it would only drive the resentment deeper. So don't swing at your mate in public. Put away slander and clamor and all malice.

And let's consider another kind of criticism: *sarcasm.* What a cruel game to play in public! And yet, it is among the favorites. Believe me, others may grin and giggle, but your mate will never forget the slam. I married a dear couple several years ago who felt so strongly against sarcasm they added to their vows a promise before God not to engage in it. Sarcasm is, indeed, an unfair swing at your mate in public. Stop it!

● ● ●

*Keep It Cleaned Up* Now the seventh rule: *When it's all over, help clean up the mess.* In verse 32 Paul gives three suggestions for mopping it up:

> And be kind to one another, tender-hearted, forgiving each other, just as God in Christ also has forgiven you.

Kindness. Tenderness. Forgiveness. At the heart of the word "kindness" is "grace." Be gracious enough to wipe it off the mental slate. At the heart of "tenderness" is "compassion." Be compassionate enough to weep with the one who's hurt from the fight.

And at the heart of forgiveness is the very person of Jesus Christ who forgave you. The greatest exhibition of forgiveness took place at Calvary. Fully forgive like He did. This clean-up process is all important.

*Keep It in Mind* Let's take a quick review of the seven rules.

1. Be committed to honesty and mutual respect.
2. Make sure the weapons are not deadly.
3. Agree that the time is right.
4. Be ready with a positive solution, soon after the swing.
5. Watch your words and guard your tone.
6. Don't swing at your mate in public.
7. When it's over, help clean up the mess. This involves kindness, tenderness, and forgiveness.

There are the rules. Write them down. Memorize them. Talk about them. But most of all . . . keep them.

## The Best Way To Stop a Fight

How do you stop most fights? Simple. When you are beaten, surrender. When you are whipped, graciously quit.

• • •

Remarkable as it seems, some adult married couples can be very poor losers. Very childish. All it takes is three monosyllabic words: "I am wrong" or "You are right." When you say this, the fight ends. Try that.

The husband comes in and he is all bent out of shape and starts to blast away.

You say, "Honey, you are right."

"What did you say?"

"You are right." Genuinely admit it and watch him melt.

Our family had a miniature schnauzer. One time this dog nearly led to a fight in our marriage. She was a female and so it came time to lock her up in the garage.

My wife said, "I really think Heidi needs to stay in the garage. I don't care if it's for a week or two weeks. We'll just have to clean up after her. That's just part of it."

I said, "I don't think that is the best plan. I think that dog needs to be outside a little. She's going to get cabin fever inside that garage. She needs to be able to enjoy being outside."

My wife said, "We're going to have trouble."

I said, "It will work out great. We'll keep our eye on her."

One Monday I was working out in the garage and she was enjoying being outside. I took a quick trip to the hardware store to get some things and when I came back I spotted a big black dog, crawling over our backyard wall with that satisfied look on his face.

I thought, "Oh, no!" I decided, "I'm not going to tell anybody anything." So I didn't. I just let it go. I said to myself, "Nothing happened. Everything is great. It's just my imagination."

And guess what. Yep. Heidi was pregnant. I had to say to my wife, "You were right. I was wrong."

• • •

And you know what? Now, it's funny. It's no longer a fight, because one of us is willing to say, "You were right." It's that simple.

You're not going to believe this, but I was in junior high school before I realized the North actually won the Civil War. In fact, some places in the South are still fighting the crazy thing. Why? It's hard for losers to give in.

As one of my close friends in Texas declares: "Those Yankees didn't win . . . we just ran out of ammunition, food, and men!"

How much better to say, "Okay, you win."

Fight all you want to, as long as you keep the rules. They will help you go on to better things. As soon as you are beaten, surrender! Only then are you able to go on.

The alternative requires turning your home into another boxing ring. And take it from me, that's no way to live. Fights belong in big, smoke-filled auditoriums, not in a house that claims to model the message of God's peace.

If you must fight, fight fair and clean. The least you can do is make it a *good* fight!

## Note

1. Sven Wahlroos, *Family Communication* (New York: Macmillan Publishing Co., 1974), p. 159.

● ● ●

# 8
. . .

# 'Til Debt Do Us Part

*L*IKE GIANT CONTAINERS of volatile gas, money *must* be handled by married couples with extreme care. Unfortunately, more often than not, our financial posture can be described in six words:

Bad mistakes

Big bills

Bank loans.

Two young adults I married over five years ago (we'll call them Ron and Becky) seemed to be an intelligent, diligent couple with above average common sense. In our premarital counseling sessions, we discussed their finances. In my standard approach, I not only warned them against over-extending themselves, but I also shared some of the principles my wife and I employ. Ron seemed to have a good handle on the subject and Becky made several comments that assured me

. . .

her head was screwed on straight. I was comfortable with the thought that the two of them would be wise and careful, employing a lot of sense with their dollars.

Becky told me recently she needed to talk with me about the growing distance between Ron and her. As she unveiled the story, I soon realized that poor money management was one of the major contributors to their disharmony.

They had wanted a home—a new one. They found their "dream" and realized quickly it was going to require a chunk of money just to get it in their name . . . plus huge monthly payments of almost $900. At 13.5 percent interest. Over and above this they planned to furnish most of the rooms, drape the windows, build a few extras in the garage, and landscape both front and back yards. Oh, yeah, they also wanted to put up a fence. They decided to finance most of those things.

Becky went to work. Ron added a second job to his busy schedule . . . and, in addition, he worked most weekends with yet another type of employment. Obviously, he was seldom home. Strangely, the very thing they wanted so badly became an empty showcase, a place to sleep, bathe, dress, and choke down a hurried breakfast. By the way, Ron left at 6:00 a.m. and dragged in around 11:30 p.m. Seven days a week. Twelve months a year. Becky was working 40 hours a week, sometimes more.

Becky got pregnant. Two weeks before delivery she quit her job. The baby increased their financial pressure, especially since it led to her unemployment. Within another eighteen months, another pregnancy.

Picture it. A weary, young mother with two in diapers. An incredibly busy husband and father, at home only between midnight and six o'clock in the morning. And that new

• • •

home neither of them has ever really enjoyed. The payments are constant. And one of the babies is currently ill. Anybody wonder why Becky and Ron are beginning to feel a distance between themselves?

Bad mistakes
Big bills
Bank loans.

## Common Problem: Mismanagement

The story can be repeated in America thousands of times. The figures and geography may differ, but not the pressure. By the way, a young executive recently told me that his house payment was *$1800 a month*. That's well over $20,000 a year just for their house. They, too, are feeling the pinch.

Small wonder one expert states that, "Nine out of every ten people with an income are financial failures." He doesn't mean they declare bankruptcy or they have bad credit or they don't make enough money. He means they fail to manage their money wisely. It's not really a question of dishonesty or lack of diligence, but rather *mismanagement.*

Candidly, I have a personal motivation for emphasizing financial wisdom in this book on marriage. A few months after we got married, Cynthia and I were living on beans and cornbread, with cornbread and syrup for dessert, partly because we had made a bad mistake in an investment. It all happened in 1955. I remember it well.

A man who advertised himself as a stockbroker had come to our area. Many of us who didn't know better were attracted to his smart appearance and his slick portfolio filled with official-looking charts, credentials, and letters of recommendation.

● ● ●

He calmly (and convincingly) explained a plan that would ultimately make us financially independent—for an initial investment of only $600. The dividends would just pour in! Well, $600 to us then would be like $15,000 today . . . but we got it! And he left town.

For good.

That was it. That crook ripped us off and split the scene. The whole deal was a fraud. One of the reasons I joined the Marine Corps shortly after that was to learn how to kill— just in case I met up with that phony some day.

But one thing good came out of our $600 mistake. We learned the value of being good stewards of our money. We discovered (the hard way) that unless we deal wisely with the finances God entrusts to our care, we will pay a terrible price. Mismanagement, quite frankly, is a sin.

## Scriptural Reproof

The Bible is a remarkable book. I continually am amazed at its breadth. When it comes to finances, it offers workable principles for living that include earning, buying, borrowing, saving, giving, and investing our money. Not even God Himself breaks these guidelines—except in a very few miraculous exceptions. Couples who wish to get their finances squared away must—I repeat, *must*—seek the counsel of Scripture. There are also some very reliable books[1] you would be wise to read and heed. But most of all, God's Word is the primary and most dependable resource to turn to.

Just listen to a few related passages on the subject of money.

Several in Proverbs are:

> A false balance is an abomination to the Lord,
> But a just weight is His delight (11:1).

● ● ●

In all labor there is profit,
But mere talk leads only to poverty (14:23).

He who profits illicitly troubles his own house,
But he who hates bribes will live (15:27).

The rich rules over the poor,
And the borrower becomes the lender's slave (22:7).

Do not weary yourself to gain wealth,
Cease from your consideration of it.
When you set your eyes on it, it is gone.
For wealth certainly makes itself wings,
Like an eagle that flies toward the heavens (23:4–5).

Know well the condition of your flocks,
And pay attention to your herds;
For riches are not forever,
Nor does a crown endure to all generations (27:23–24).

Solomon also wrote:

He who loves money will not be satisfied with money,
nor he who loves abundance with its income. This too is
vanity.

ECCLESIASTES 5:10

Jesus said these familiar words:

Then the Pharisees went and counseled together how
they might trap Him in what He said.

And they sent their disciples to Him, along with the
Herodians, saying, "Teacher, we know that You are
truthful and teach the way of God in truth, and defer to
no one; for You are not partial to any."

• • •

"Tell us therefore, what do You think? Is it lawful to give a poll-tax to Caesar, or not?"

But Jesus perceived their malice, and said, "Why are you testing Me, you hypocrites?"

"Show Me the coin used for the poll-tax." And they brought Him a denarius.

And He said to them, "Whose likeness and inscription is this?"

They said to Him, "Caesar's." Then He said to them, "Then render to Caesar the things that are Caesar's; and to God the things that are God's."

And hearing this, they marveled, and leaving Him, they went away.

MATTHEW 22:15–22

And Paul added:

For because of this you also pay taxes, for rulers are servants of God, devoting themselves to this very thing.

Render to all what is due them: tax to whom tax is due; custom to whom custom; fear to whom fear; honor to whom honor.

Owe nothing to anyone except to love one another; for he who loves his neighbor has fulfilled the law.

ROMANS 13:6–8

and,

Now this I say, he who sows sparingly shall also reap sparingly; and he who sows bountifully shall also reap bountifully.

Let each one do just as he has purposed in his heart; not grudgingly or under compulsion; for God loves a cheerful giver.

• • •

And God is able to make all grace abound to you, that always having all sufficiency in everything, you may have an abundance for every good deed.

2 CORINTHIANS 9:6–8

And finally,

And if we have food and covering, with these we shall be content.

But those who want to get rich fall into temptation and a snare and many foolish and harmful desires which plunge men into ruin and destruction.

For the love of money is a root of all sorts of evil, and some by longing for it have wandered away from the faith, and pierced themselves with many a pang.

Instruct those who are rich in this present world not to be conceited or to fix their hope on the uncertainty of riches, but on God, who richly supplies us with all things to enjoy.

Instruct them to do good, to be rich in good works, to be generous and ready to share,

storing up for themselves the treasure of a good foundation for the future, so that they may take hold of that which is life indeed.

1 TIMOTHY 6:8–10, 17–19

## Seven Wrong Attitudes

As I think deeply about those great statements from God's Book and then call to mind the attitudes I have witnessed among married couples I have talked to, what a contrast! If I were to summarize them into a list, I believe I could name seven attitudes commonly found in Christian homes:

1. That part is God's money; this part is mine.
2. God really isn't concerned with "secular" things.

● ● ●

3. Let's not get fanatical. Leave God at church.
4. Financial prosperity is suspect—profit-making is unspiritual.
5. Having little is more spiritual than having much.
6. Don't sweat it, some day our ship will come in.
7. God isn't fair! The rich get richer and the poor get poorer.

All seven are wrong.

Not one of these attitudes squares with Scripture. Any marriage that operates from one or more of these concepts is headed either for trouble or, at best, for less than God has designed for us to enjoy.

## A Relevant Parable for Today

Several years ago God opened my eyes to a passage of Scripture in Luke 19 that has really helped me to view the management of my finances as *He* views it. This passage is a parable Jesus spoke regarding a prophetic issue I won't get into—I'll just deal with its insights related to money. As we'll see, it offers seven facts that correct the wrong attitudes we just considered.

I have in mind Luke 19:11–26. To set the stage, let's read verses 11–12 first. I'll use the New International Version for the sake of clarity:

> While they were listening to this, he went on to tell them a parable, because he was near Jerusalem and the people thought that the kingdom of God was going to appear at once. He said:
> "A man of noble birth went to a distant country to have himself appointed king and then to return. So he called ten of his servants and gave them ten minas. 'Put this money to work,' he said, 'until I come back.'"

● ● ●

Obviously, His own departure and return were in Jesus' mind. That prophetic thought is woven throughout the parable. He is the "man of noble birth" and the servants we are going to read about are His followers, people like you and me. So much for the prophetic part—now let's zero in on the practical.

### Managing God's Money

"So he called ten of his servants and gave them ten minas. 'Put this money to work,' he said, 'until I come back'" (v. 13).

Here's the first fact that counteracts the wrong attitude I mentioned earlier—

*Everything we have has come from God.*

This verse states He gave them all the money they were to have. By the way, a "mina" was about three months' wages. Being servants, they possessed nothing apart from the nobleman's provision. Nothing. Servants in those days were totally dependent upon their masters for everything.

You and I are like that. It is incorrect to think that our part is the whole thing minus God's part. No way. Everything we possess, from the coins in our pockets to the savings in the bank, belong to Him. In actuality, the Christian doesn't "own" anything. He or she simply manages God's money. What we handle is entrusted to us from God's hand. This is basic. You will never get a handle on a proper (biblical) perspective of your finances, my friend, until you grasp this foundational fact.

### Destroying Secular-Sacred Distinctions  Now, back to the story. After giving each servant the same amount of money, He told them, "Put this money to work . . . until I come

• • •

back." The Greek verb conveys the idea of "doing business." It is *pragmateuomai,* from which we get "pragmatic." It's a practical, pragmatic command. "Carry on with business until I get back."

Second fact: *In God's eyes, there is no "secular" and "sacred" distinction.*

It is totally inaccurate for you and your marriage partner to think that your business life (stuff that occurs outside church affairs) is of little or no interest to God. When our Lord says "do business," He doesn't mention categories. All of our dealings are of utmost interest to our Lord.

It's wise mentally to "ordain" everything to Him and His service. If you're a teacher, you're an "ordained teacher." A homemaker? Then you're an "ordained homemaker." If you are thinking about investing in something, view that as an "ordained investment."

Why? Because it is His money. And you are carrying on business for Him. The Lord is extremely interested in how we do business. How we budget, how we plan, spend, and save. We are to be as adept in keeping our books as we are in preaching and teaching His Word. He is equally as interested in the way we handle the payroll in our private business as He is in the way we handle His Word. There's no secular-sacred distinction. Remember that!

### Doing Business God's Way  Let's read on:

> "But his subjects hated him and sent a delegation after him to say, 'We don't want this man to be our king'"
> (v. 14).

Fact three is clear:
*Doing business God's way is contrary to man's way.*

• • •

The citizens mentioned here are not to be confused with His servants. They represent the inbred worldliness in all of us. You know, that part of us that craves selfish satisfaction. Doing our own thing our own way.

In this parable these subjects said they didn't want His lordship. "We hate Him—we resent His trying to control this part of our lives. This is *our* business!"

Sound familiar? Perhaps you feel like that. You may read this book from cover to cover and intellectually agree with the principles it sets forth. But deep down in your soul—down where those gutsy decisions are made—you really don't have any plans to change your comfortable, present habit patterns. You don't want Him to be your King and to reign over you. You just want to get what you want out of life. Let me level with you. That is rebellion and resistance. It's carnality in the raw. And I can assure you your marriage will not improve until you submit to him.

When he returns, the nobleman asks his slaves, "How did things go?" Look at verse 15:

> "He was made king, however, and returned home.
> Then he sent for the servants to whom he had given the
> money, in order to find out what they had gained with
> it" (v. 15).

What was the nobleman concerned about? Business. He wasn't concerned about differences or divisions in segments of the land. He wanted to know, "How was business? Were you wise in managing the money?" Then look at the response in verse 16:

> "The first one came and said, 'Sir, your mina has
> earned ten more'" (v. 16).

● ● ●

Underline the word "your." Not "my" mina, Lord, but *yours.* "Lord, Your salary provided this. Your financial provision for promotion made this possible for us as a family. Lord, your money has prospered me in this way and as I stand before You, here's my accounting of it."

> "'Well done, my good servant!' his master replied. 'Because you have been trustworthy in a very small matter, take charge of ten cities'" (v. 17).

What a tremendous reward!

### Pleasing God with Money Management

> "The second came and said, 'Sir, your mina has earned five more'" (v. 18).

A mina was worth about $20. By wise investment he turned his $20 into $100. Another reward: authority over five cities.

The master was pleased with the servant's initiative, which introduces the fourth fact:

*Wise management of money pleases the Lord.*

Some "superspiritual saints" spread rumors that financial success is suspect. They say profit-making is unspiritual. I cannot find a biblical basis for that. Certainly, how we use it is important, but making it is not, in and of itself, unspiritual. This nobleman came back and asked, "What did you do?"

"I earned more than you gave me."

"Wonderful. Ten cities are for you."

It seems obvious to me he was pleased with the profit.

We have to be careful what that profit means to us. We're not to amass fortunes for ourselves, to hang on, look at,

• • •

love, and selfishly enjoy. Earlier in this chapter, we read warnings from both Solomon and Paul.

Rather, should fortune come, we are to be willing to turn around and give it away. That's the difference. The selfish man gets it so that he might keep it. The born-again individual gets it so that he might release it to those in need . . . and wisely invest it in so many other areas.

I've said all my life, and I believe it more now than ever, that the happiest people on planet earth are not the keepers. They are the givers. The man who received a mina and through wise management earned tenfold pleased his lord. And the nobleman turned right around and rewarded him. Wouldn't God do the same with us?

***Displeasing God Without Money Management*** There is one more slave to report in:

> "Then another servant came and said, 'Sir, here is your mina; I have kept it laid away in a piece of cloth. I was afraid of you, because you are a hard man. You take out what you did not put in and reap what you did not sow.'
>
> "His master replied, 'I will judge you by your own words, you wicked servant!'" (vv. 20–22).

Wait a minute, nobleman. He didn't lose it, he's still got it. The one that had $20 wound up with the same $20 later. But the Lord says, "That's not wise," meaning, "I'm not pleased that you just sat on it. I expect you to invest it so it increases in value."

The man had his excuse ready: "I was afraid of you, lord." But his excuse didn't hold water.

Through this slave we find the fifth fact:

• • •

*Poor management displeases the Lord.*

This dispels the common attitude that having little is more spiritual than having much. Where is that idea found in the Bible? Or the thought that God loves the poor more than He loves the rich? I don't believe that. Having riches carries with it a temptation and responsibility the poor never wrestle with. But nowhere in Scripture do I find that being financially prosperous is unspiritual.

**Disciplining Your Investment Efforts**    Notice what the nobleman asks next:

> "'Why then didn't you put my money on deposit, so that when I came back, I could have collected it with interest?'" (v. 23).

That's a good question, isn't it? The Lord offers a low-risk alternative to doing nothing: putting it in a bank so that the principal earns interest. That brings us to the sixth fact:

*Management and disciplined planning go hand-in-hand.*
An investment plan takes discipline to maintain. And discipline without a plan is frustration. They go together.

That means ignorance is *not* bliss. We can't sigh, "Some day our ship will come in." We can't close our eyes and put it on the credit card. READ THAT SENTENCE AGAIN.

By the way, I'm not against credit. I understand that our economy is such that we would be in trouble without credit. I don't understand all that I should about economics, but I do understand that the interest factor works in our favor when properly held in check. My great concern is the unwise overspending so many couples carry on that breaks their relationship and reveals poor discipline. Here the Lord says,

• • •

"Look, the least you could have done is deposit it in the bank so it could draw interest."

*Losing and Learning*   Now, look closely at the following two verses:

> "Then he said to those standing by, 'Take his mina away from him and give it to the one who has ten minas."
> "'Sir,' they said, 'he already has ten!'" (vv. 24–25).

Does that seem fair? He's giving it to the fellow who already has a lot! But the Lord says:

> "'I tell you that to everyone who has, more will be given, but as for the one who has nothing, even what he has will be taken away'"(v. 26).

I believe this shows that God blesses wise management, but poor management sees dwindling returns. This seventh fact is the most difficult:

*Losses and gains provide eternal lessons.*

Our problem is that we don't learn our lessons when we lose or gain. We live in some kind of spiritual dream world, thinking that somehow, in some marvelous way, it's all going to float down in our favor. But God has devised laws and principles for living which include spending, buying, borrowing, saving, and investing.

## Learning, Earning, Yearning

The book of Proverbs is filled with maxims about the wisdom of the diligent man. Many of those proverbs imply wisdom in money management. The disciplined, diligent man will be blessed. The one who lacks diligence will become the

• • •

slave of the lender. (Look again at Proverbs 22:7.) This applies to us when we're earning the least money of our lives and when we've hit our peak earning period. In fact, our earning power could be graphed as a semicircle, low when we're 20 to 30 years of age, rising to a peak in the middle years, and slacking off in retirement.[2]

*Figure 1.* **Financial Lifeline**

| Learning Period | Earning Period *Years of Accumulation* | Yearning Period |
|---|---|---|
| Small Earning Power | Peak of Earning Power | Small Earning Power |
| 20  25  30  35  40  45  50  55  60  65 | | |
| 40  35  30  25  20  15  10  5  0  0 | | |
| Years left in which to complete the job | | |

Let's call that first period of earning power the "learning period." One of the great breakdowns in our society is the failure of parents to teach their children how to manage their money. Maybe parents will pass on a couple of important lessons they've learned (believe me, my kids have heard the story of my "investment" enough times!), but they don't ground their children well in basic financial planning.

Our earning power also shrinks when we're 60 or older. Call this the "yearning period."

In the middle of life, ages 30 to 60, we reach the peak. This is our "earning period." Think, though, of your age in

• • •

terms of how many years you have left to plan wisely for your family, parents. When you are 20, you have 40 years left. When you're 30, just as you're moving into the higher-income time, you have only 30 years left. When you hit 40, you have 20 years left. By the time you've reached 50, there are 10 years (give or take a few) left to plan those investments.

Only the Lord knows how set in concrete we really are by the age of 45 or 50 to rethink our finances. You don't have an eternity ahead of you to plan these things. Everything may seem terribly spiritual until suddenly a man leaves a widow and a bunch of children, with no financial assistance. When she is jolted back to reality, she knows they should have planned. As a pastor who ministers to the dying and the grieving, I see this often.

## The Bible and Financial Planning

I find four scriptural principles for financial planning. The first is tucked away between the lines of Matthew 22:15–22:

> Then the Pharisees went and counseled together how they might trap Him in what He said.
>
> And they sent their disciples to Him, along with the Herodians, saying, "Teacher, we know that You are truthful and teach the way of God in truth, and defer to no one; for You are not partial to any.
>
> "Tell us therefore, what do You think? Is it lawful to give a poll-tax to Caesar, or not?"
>
> But Jesus perceived their malice, and said, "Why are you testing Me, you hypocrites?
>
> "Show Me the coin used for the poll-tax." And they brought Him a denarius (vv. 15–19).

● ● ●

That little denarius they held up in front of His face was smaller than an American quarter, though worth about a day's wages. Jesus looked at the impression on the coin and said, "Whose likeness and inscription is this?" What's stamped on this coin?

> They said to Him, "Caesar's." Then He said to them,
> "Then render to Caesar the things that are Caesar's; and
> to God the things that are God's" (v. 21).

Pay your taxes if you are deriving benefit from the government, but give God the things that are God's. Simple answer. Let's look at the implications.

***On Taxes and Tithes*** It's interesting that this passage is always used to describe the biblical necessity of paying one's taxes. But we seldom have someone emphasize the ending of the sentence about rendering to God the things that are God's. We live and die by the joke that nothing is really certain in life except taxes and death. But there *is* something else. God's part. We are to "render," he says, which means "pay back." The Greek verb means "to return." Remember that primary axiom? Everything we have is *His*. Just as we are to pay taxes and just as we must die, we must also give God His part.

The first principle here is: *Christ and Caesar are essential, not optional.* You can't live very long in this world without paying taxes. If you try to ignore them, they catch up with you. The same is true of the Lord's part. If you are involved in a church and deriving a major benefit from it for your family or your own life, then the majority of your contribution should go there.

Often people give as though they were serving out pump-

● ● ●

kin pie. They cut up their giving into a number of different pieces and a small part winds up in the church. But the rest is sent elsewhere. Some of that certainly is appropriate. That's the only way many needy ministries could continue. My concern is with the optional feeling many people have toward giving to the local church.

We never think of taxes as optional; Caesar gets his part. But Christ is also to get His part and it is to be planned for. Carefully. Thoroughly. Consistently. Yet how often, when the plate's being passed, do we dig hastily into our pockets and grab something to drop in? At the same time I know men who spend hours and days planning ways to reduce their taxes.

God's part also needs time to be planned out. After all, He is to take first place in our life (Colossians 1:18). The benefits and blessings that are derived are incredible and can never be paid back. Christian couple—give God His part!

*Back-to-Back Borrowing*   The second principle comes from Romans 13:6–8, a passage I've wrestled with for a long time:

> For because of this you also pay taxes, for rulers are servants of God, devoting themselves to this very thing.
> Render to all what is due them: tax to whom tax is due; custom to whom custom; fear to whom fear; honor to whom honor.
> Owe nothing to anyone except to love one another; for he who loves his neighbor has fulfilled the law.

I have debts, as you have debts, yet verse 8 said that I am to owe nothing to anyone except to love him. I've been tempted at times just to send our creditors some notes saying, "I love you very much." With no remittance enclosed. Some-

● ● ●

how, I don't think they would accept my love note as a substitute.

"Owe nothing to anyone except to love one another." What does that mean? Is it wrong for a couple to invest and borrow for a home or some large expenditure? Or take out small loans? When Dallas Theological Seminary was making expansion plans, I talked with its president, Dr. John F. Walvoord, about this very point. His answer was a wise one.

"If you look closely," this president-scholar said, "you will notice that the imperative is in the present tense. The thought is 'don't keep on owing.'"

In other words, don't stack up your loans back-to-back so that you never have a break. Pay them off. Don't prolong the debt. Hence the second principle:

*Buying and borrowing demand short accounts, not long ones.*

Nothing needs to be watched more closely than credit buying. In my premarital counseling with couples I mentioned earlier, one of our sessions deals with the matter of not getting head over heels in debt. Some couples stack up the bills before the knot is even tied with elaborate and expensive plans. These quickly plunge them into the financial pits and soon they have thousands of dollars of "wants" overwhelming them. The only solution is to insist on short accounts.

***"Saving Up" Instead of "Dreaming On"*** The third principle is that *savings and security require planning, not dreaming.* Proverbs 14:23 says:

> In all labor there is profit, but mere talk leads only to poverty.

● ● ●

If you want a savings account to build up security for investment, don't just talk and dream about it. A plan will never come to fruition unless it is put into operation.

My wife and I are working toward aligning our family budget according to the guidelines in figure 2. Your total earnings are represented on the top. Out of the total earnings, the Lord is first, then comes taxes to the government. That which remains is what I call the "working money." From there, allow 10 percent for savings and investments, 70 percent for living expenses, and 20 percent for debts and a buffer fund to handle those unexpected items.

I am indebted to Bowman's book *How to Succeed With Your Money* and for his excellent suggestions for working within this framework.[3] You might also seek financial advice from someone you respect, such as your banker. Go to men of integrity whose expertise is money and investment. You'll be wiser to seek their counsel, because savings and securities need intelligent planning, not hopeful dreaming.

*Figure 2.* **A Suggested Financial Formula***

| TOTAL EARNINGS | | | |
| --- | --- | --- | --- |
| | WORKING MONEY | | |
| THE LORD | 10% | 70% | 20% |
| | • Savings & Investment | | Debts & • Buffer Fund |
| GOVERNMENT | | • Living Expenses | |

* The "10-70-20" Plan

• • •

*How Much Is Too Much?*   The fourth and final principle of financial planning is this:

*Things and treasures are temporal, not eternal.*

Paul's first letter to Timothy tells why:

> And if we have food and covering, with these we shall be content (6:8).

It will help emphasize the truth if you will change the word "shall" to "should." That would be more realistic. Having food and covering, we *should* be content. Alas, we often are not. We start thinking our treasures will last forever and we want to pile them up.

> But those who want to get rich fall into temptation and a snare and many foolish and harmful desires which plunge men into ruin and destruction. For the love of money is a root of all sorts of evil.
>
> 1 TIMOTHY 6:9–10

Money is not evil, but the love of it—the idolatry of the coin—is.

Born-again, wealthy people whose hearts are right, however, are to be generous and ready to share—

> ... storing up for themselves the treasure of a good foundation for the future, so that they may take hold of that which is life indeed.
>
> 1 TIMOTHY 6:19

"Life indeed," if I could paraphrase, is "really living." The man, woman, or couple occupied only with money, money, money have missed what it really means to live.

Well, that's it. Big subject, isn't it? Lots to think about. But

• • •

if we don't, our marriages suffer. In fact, many of them will fail.

I wish someone would have pulled me aside twenty-five years ago and helped me understand these things. Really! Maybe that's why I've written such a long chapter . . . to keep you from struggling as much as I have with finances.

Now that I've got a biblical handle on the subject, I am much more at ease, much less fearful. Alas, for many couples, however, long before death separates them, debts will.

It need not be.

## Notes

1. I have found a great deal of help from four particular books. All four are based on scriptural principles and therefore are reliable resources to consider: *How to Succeed with Your Money,* George M. Bowman, Moody Press; *You Can Be Financially Free,* George Fooshee, Jr., Fleming H. Revell Company; *Handbook for Financial Faithfulness,* Floyd Sharp and Al Macdonald, Zondervan Publishing House; *Your Money: Frustration or Freedom?* Howard L. Dayton, Jr., Tyndale House Publishers, Inc.

2. George M. Bowman, *How to Succeed with Your Money* (Chicago: Moody Press, 1960), p. 71.

3. Ibid., p. 129.

● ● ●

# 9
## ...

# Divorce: When It All Comes Tumbling Down

**U**P 'TIL NOW, this has been an enjoyable book to write.

We've consulted the Architect of the home and discovered His original blueprint for getting it all together. We've repaired the foundation by returning to that great passage in Genesis 2 and learning about severance, permanence, unity, and intimacy. We have studied about those necessary bricks that build a marriage, how to keep our honeymoon from ending, ways to handle our conflicts, and even some tips on wise money management.

Written across every page has been the word HOPE. We have openly admitted our imperfections and we have willingly declared our need for divine assistance. Every major point and principle have been affirmed by Scripture . . . so we have not built a case on human opinion. Time and again

## . . .

we have returned to the "original match" to analyze, compare, observe, and learn. We have been reassured that there is no marital problem so great that God cannot solve it. Rebuilding and rekindling have been the recurring theme. No marriage—no matter how weak or scarred—need end.

I again agree with my friend in San Francisco. Two processes ought never be entered into prematurely: embalming and divorce. Time and again I have suggested ways in which a marriage can be salvaged. Because I firmly believe there is *nothing* impossible with God. Because I have seen Him turn numerous husbands and wives around—180 degrees. Because it was never His original design that homes be destroyed. And because His Word is filled with promises that hold out hope to those who have blown it. But. . . .

Divorce still occurs. Now, more than ever. Often against the desire of one of the partners. Often in spite of assistance, effort, and much prayer by friends. Often between two Christians—yes, often. And always where biblical principles were unknown, ignored, or openly violated. Nevertheless, divorce happens. It's a fact we may hate (I confess, I really do!), but one we cannot deny.

And so, instead of dodging divorce and acting like it's not there, I've decided to write a chapter that faces it squarely. Even though I would much prefer not to, I haven't that option.

I will be brief (there are entire *books* written on the subject), biblical, and compassionate. But in spite of these efforts, I'm sure some of you will be offended and others will misunderstand. Such is inevitable, unfortunately.

## A Controversial Subject

I'm convinced that there is no way any group of Christians picked at random would ever come to unanimity on

● ● ●

this subject. I'll go further. I don't believe a bus load of American evangelical theologians would be in unanimous agreement on divorce and remarriage even if they toured the United States an entire summer! It's a controversial issue, for sure. Therefore, no matter what I may conclude, I am confident some very reliable, competent, and equally sincere people will disagree. So save your cards and letters!

I am also confident of this. It's time some of us in the evangelical camp came up front and addressed the issue boldly. Many a divorced person is grinding out his or her life under an enormous load of unnecessary guilt. While I certainly would not desire to soften the penetrating blows of the Spirit of God (if, in fact, it *is* the Spirit producing conviction), I do hope that my words provide the breathing room God has allowed in certain instances. Of greatest concern to me is that someone might read these pages and *misinterpret* what I am saying. Disagreement is one thing; misinterpretation is another. And the emotions surrounding something as stressful as divorce have a way of playing tricks on one's mind, increasing the possibility of misinterpreting what one reads.

Let's make a deal. I promise to be as accurate, clear, and concise as I can possibly be with what I write if you will be equally as careful with what you read. Work hard at not reading into this something I am not saying . . . or take to an extreme something I am trying to keep in proper balance. In issues as controversial as this one, the vehicle of communication must be finely tuned. Let's both do our part, okay?

## Not in God's Original Blueprint

It should surprise no one that divorce was never in the original blueprint for the home. Not only is that implied in the Genesis account, it is clearly stated by Jesus:

• • •

> "Because of your hardness of heart, Moses permitted
> you to divorce your wives; but *from the beginning it has
> not been this way* [emphasis mine].
>
> MATTHEW 19:8

The original match was simple and clear: one man (Adam) with one woman (Eve) joined together in a permanent union (marriage) throughout life. How perfect! Yes, and how innocent! Remember, sin was not yet present. Nor a carnal nature within human life. In the beginning days of the home, (think of it!), there was absolute perfection.

Man was totally innocent. Uncontaminated. As we read in Genesis 5:1–2:

> . . . In the day when God created man, He made him
> in the likeness of God.
> He created them male and female, and He blessed
> them and named them Man in the day when they were
> created.

Clear enough, isn't it? Sinlessness. God's likeness infused into two human beings. The very image of God was stamped upon His creation.

## Sin's Shattering Effect on Marriage

But wait. Read on. In the same chapter, the very next verse, this is recorded:

> When Adam had lived one hundred and thirty years,
> he became the father of a son in his own likeness, accord-
> ing to his image, and named him Seth.

Notice the difference? The dad had originally been created in God's likeness, but when Seth came along, he was in Adam's likeness—"according to his (his father's) image." Why? Sin

● ● ●

had invaded. Genesis 3 tells the grim story. And with the invasion of sin came all its horrible consequences, not the least of which was the beginning of strife, both internal (the root) and external (the fruit).

The disease impacted everything and everyone. Conflict replaced harmony. War replaced peace. Sorrow replaced joy. And things like disobedience, rebellion, argumentation, and even murder became the status quo. In nations. In cities. And in homes as well. Yes, marriages were not exempt. Unlike the original match, husbands and wives became selfish, demanding, brutal, unfaithful, angry, hateful, and competitive.

The nation Israel, God's chosen people, ultimately began to lose their distinction. They ignored God's directions and intermarried with foreigners—non-Israelites. The Jew-Gentile mixture was more than God would allow . . . so a compromise was provided by Moses. A "certificate of divorce" (Deuteronomy 24:1–4) was permitted due to the rampant epidemic that was threatening the uniqueness of Israel. Because of the stubborn, rebellious will of sinful people— Jesus called it "hardness of heart"—divorce evolved. But remember, it was not desired or designed in God's original arrangement for marriage. Sin polluted the plan.

Let's see if I can illustrate the problem another way. Pretend you and your family save enough money to buy a swimming pool. You meet with a builder and you discuss your design preferences. He smiles as he watches you sign the contract and give him your first check. The hole is dug, the reinforcement steel is installed, the cement is blown in, the plaster and tile are finished, and everybody is ecstatic. He kept his word and you paid the bill. Now, of course, the water needs to be added. As the pool begins to fill up, a strange color appears before your eyes—Green. Not crystal

• • •

clear . . . not even bright blue. No, it's green. And the longer you watch, the greener it gets!

Now, you never intended to have green water. You envisioned a sparkling, clear, inviting pool . . . that was your original plan. But an enemy has come without invitation. Germs. And the longer that enemy stays, uncontested, the more putrid the pool appears. So you must make a concession. A compromise is essential, unless you choose to fill up the pool with dirt and forget all about swimming. You must add chemicals. Chlorine and acid and other materials must be placed into your lovely, once-white-and-ideal pool. They will burn your eyes and bleach your swimsuit . . . but if you're going to have a pool at all, chemicals must be used to counteract the germs. Like it or not (and you don't), you must compromise with the original plan.

And so it is with marriage. Because of the harsh presence and consequences of sin, divorce was permitted, lest marriage and the distinctives of a home that modeled Jehovah's character be completely nullified and destroyed. In that sense, divorce became a way of salvaging the believer's distinctives. But remember—it was never God's original intention or desire. It was permitted once the ravages of sinfulness reached threatening proportions.

## When Is It Acceptable To Remarry?

Enough of history. Let's come to the present. The question everyone wants answered is this: When is divorce permissible? Because of limited time and space, I will spare you a lot of verbiage and supportive quotations. Suffice it to say, I will answer the question with remarriage in mind. In other words, my answers assume that we are really asking, "Are there any biblical grounds for remarriage?"

• • •

I believe there are. I have searched the Scriptures, read everything I can get my hands on, and discussed this issue with my wife, my friends, fellow staff, and church board members, pastors, many theological professors, and other serious students of the Bible. I have talked with numerous divorced people, single persons, married couples, publishers, authors on the subject, and authorities in the field—both Christian and non-Christian. Here are my conclusions, simplified for the sake of clarity.

I believe the Christian has biblical grounds for remarriage when the divorce transpired under one of the three situations described in the following pages.

***A Marriage and Divorce Prior to Salvation***   1. *When the marriage and divorce occurred prior to salvation.*

In 2 Corinthians 5:17 we read these words:

> Therefore if any man is in Christ, he is a new creature;
> the old things passed away; behold, new things have
> come.

I take this literally. I even take it to the extreme! I think "new" means "new." . . . So when God promises the believing sinner that He is "a new creature," then I take that to mean exactly that. A brand new, fresh creation. Unlike before.

> The Greek term, *kainos,* means . . . "that which is
> unaccustomed or unused, not new in time, recent, but
> new as to form or quality, of different nature from what
> is contrasted as old."[1]

"Fresh" would be an acceptable synonym. It is used in the New Testament to describe Christ's "new commandment" to

• • •

His disciples (John 13:34), the "new covenant" (Matthew 26:28–29), the sinner being made a "new man" (Ephesians 2:15), having a "new self" (Ephesians 4:24), our being given a "new name" in heaven (Revelation 2:17), and the "new heaven and a new earth" John the apostle saw (Revelation 21:1).

There can be no question about it, this has in mind the brand new, fresh, unused creature one becomes at the moment of salvation. And if that isn't enough, Paul goes on to add "the old things passed away" at that same time. Again, I take that literally. The old life, with all its old characteristics and sins. They are, in grace, removed. The best word is *forgiven*. Totally and completely.

If that seems too extreme for you, perhaps it would help to read, slowly, those opening words in Ephesians 2:

> And you were dead in your trespasses and sins, in which you formerly walked according to the course of this world, according to the prince of the power of the air, of the spirit that is now working in the sons of disobedience.
>
> Among them we too all formerly lived in the lusts of our flesh, indulging the desires of the flesh and of the mind, and were by nature children of wrath, even as the rest.
>
> But God, being rich in mercy, because of His great love with which He loved us,
> even when we were dead in our transgressions, made us alive together with Christ (by grace you have been saved),
> and raised us up with Him, and seated us with Him in the heavenly places, in Christ Jesus,

● ● ●

> in order that in the ages to come He might show the
> surpassing riches of His grace in kindness toward us in
> Christ Jesus (vv. 1–7).

and just a few verses later in the same chapter:

> So then you are no longer strangers and aliens, but
> you are fellow citizens with the saints, and are of God's
> household,
> having been built upon the foundation of the apostles
> and prophets, Christ Jesus Himself being the corner
> stone,
> in whom the whole building, being fitted together is
> growing into a holy temple in the Lord;
> in whom you also are being built together into a
> dwelling of God in the Spirit (vv. 19–22).

Quite frankly, it is beyond my comprehension that passages such as these (there are dozens more) exclude divorce. If they do, then divorce is the only sin not covered by the blood of Christ. It is the one, permanent spot in our past that cannot be washed away. Furthermore, it is then questionable that we can take the words of David at face value when he writes:

> He has not dealt with us according to our sins,
> Nor rewarded us according to our iniquities.
> For as high as the heavens are above the earth,
> So great is His lovingkindness toward those who fear Him.
> As far as the east is from the west,
> So far has He removed our transgressions from us.
> Psalm 103:10–12

No, I believe "new" means "new." And when God promises the passing away of "old things," it surely includes

● ● ●

divorce prior to salvation. After all, being alienated from God and at enmity with Him, how could any unbeliever possibly know His will regarding the choice of a lifetime mate? Having thought through this very carefully, I believe it falls within the context of God's superabundant grace to wipe our slate clean when we turn, by faith, to Christ the Lord.

When the marriage and divorce occurred prior to salvation, I believe God grants His "new creation" the freedom to remarry.

***An Immoral and Unrepentant Partner*** 2. *When one's mate is guilty of sexual immorality and is unwilling to repent and live faithfully with the marriage partner.*

Much has been written on this particular issue, I realize. I repeat, I have read everything I can get my hands on, so I do not write these words hurriedly or superficially. I am fully aware of the difficulties connected with determining who is really the guilty party when it comes to sexual promiscuity. I also acknowledge the subjectivity involved in identifying "sexual immorality." Such matters must be carefully determined, usually with the help of a qualified counselor who can provide objectivity and wisdom in matters this serious. Each case *must* be considered independently.

Nevertheless, we cannot ignore or deny what Christ said in Matthew 19:9:

> "And I say to you, whoever divorces his wife, except for immorality, and marries another woman commits adultery."

All sorts of interpretations have been suggested to explain what our Lord was saying. Frankly, having examined every one of the suggestions and theories (some of them are incred-

• • •

ibly forced and complicated), I return to the verse and accept it at face value.

Throughout my Christian life I have operated under a very simple—yet reliable—principle of interpretation:

*If the normal sense makes good sense, seek no other sense.*

Let's do that here. Jesus is answering a question (it's in verse 3) asked by some Pharisees. It's a question related to divorce:

> "Is it lawful for a man to divorce his wife for any cause at all?"

This leads to a second question (v. 7) having to do with the reason divorce was permitted in the first place:

> "Why then did Moses command to give her a certificate and divorce her?"

His answer is clear:

> He said to them, "Because of your hardness of heart, Moses permitted you to divorce your wives; but from the beginning it has not been this way."

And then, to clarify the matter even further, He adds:

> "And I say to you, whoever divorces his wife, except for immorality, and marries another woman commits adultery."

This is Christ's personal counsel regarding justification for divorce and remarriage. That is the "normal sense" of the verse, hence we need not seek any other sense. The only thing that might help is to understand the meaning of the original term translated "immorality."

It is the Greek word *porneia,* from which we get the term

• • •

"pornography." Throughout the New Testament it is used repeatedly as a term to describe illicit sexual activity. In the case of married partners, it would refer to intimate sexual involvement with someone other than one's mate—someone either of the opposite (heterosexual infidelity) or of the same sex (homosexual activity).

Our Lord has reaffirmed that in the beginning (Adam and Eve in the Garden of Eden), divorce was not present. But due to the "hardness of heart" permission was granted to allow divorce. Jesus spells out in detail when such a divorce and remarriage would be acceptable. When a spouse is guilty of immoral sexual conduct with another person and is unwilling to remain faithful to the innocent partner, the option is there for the faithful mate to divorce and remarry.

Before moving on to the third reason, let me ask you to reread that last sentence. I want to amplify it for a few moments. Two thoughts need to be emphasized. First, this is not simply a case of quickie sex on the sly—a one-time-only experience. This is *porneia*. I take this to mean an immorality that suggests a sustained unwillingness to remain faithful. I hesitate to use the term lest I be misinterpreted—but I think of the idea of an immoral *life style,* an obvious determination to practice a promiscuous relationship outside the bonds of marriage.

Second, the faithful mate has the *option* to leave . . . but such is not mandatory. I have seen numerous marriages rebuilt rather than ended because the faithful partner had no inner peace pursuing a divorce. How much better to look for ways to make the marriage work rather than anxiously anticipate evidence that is needed to break off the relationship. But there are occasions when every attempt has been made to keep the marriage together . . . but sustained sexual

● ● ●

infidelity won't allow it. It is in such cases our Lord grants freedom from that miserable and unbearable bond.

**Desertion by an Unbeliever**  3. *When one of the mates is an unbeliever and willfully and permanently deserts the believing partner.*

In order for us to understand this, we need to read 1 Corinthians 7:12–15 very carefully.

> But to the rest I say, not the Lord, that if any brother *[a Christian]* has a wife who is an unbeliever *[a non-Christian]*, and she consents to live with him, let him not send her away.
>
> And a woman *[a Christian]* who has an unbelieving husband *[a non-Christian]*, and he consents to live with her, let her not send her  husband away.
>
> For the unbelieving husband is sanctified through his wife, and the unbelieving wife is sanctified through her believing husband; for otherwise your children are unclean, but now they are holy.
>
> Yet if the unbelieving one *[a non-Christian]* leaves, let him leave; the brother or the sister *[a Christian]* is not under bondage in such cases, but God has called us to peace *[brackets mine]*.

Paul is giving sound advice on marriage. He is offering counsel nowhere else revealed in Scripture. This passage is unique in that it addresses the very common problem of a mixed marriage, i.e., one partner is a Christian, the other is not. Interestingly, the counsel does not assume that such marriages are always unbearable. On the contrary, there are times when harmony and compatibility (to an extent) are possible. In such cases the Christian is strictly forbidden to

● ● ●

walk away from the marriage. If the unbeliever desires to remain—stay put!

But there are occasions when "the unbelieving one leaves." *Please* take note that he or she is not forced out. No, the non-Christian mate willfully deserts, walks out, refuses to stay, chooses to leave. What's God's counsel to the Christian who is left? ". . . let him leave." In other words, the Christian is not under obligation to plead, to beg, to bargain, or to force the non-Christian partner to remain. Rather, ". . . let him leave."

But that is not the end of this counsel. Verse 15 goes on to say:

> . . . the brother or sister is not under bondage in such cases. . . .

Of course, the key phrase is "not under bondage." Its meaning? Well, at the root of the Greek term is *doulos,* the New Testament term for "slave." Slaves were bound to their masters, inseparably linked to them. It is a strong word suggesting a firm, solid tie. I'm reminded of the verse in Genesis 2 that says the man "cleaves" to his wife. Remember, that word means "glue." Paul clearly has the marriage bond in mind here. Later in the chapter, he refers to this bond as being terminated at the death of one's mate:

> A wife is **bound** as long as her husband lives; but if her husband is dead, she is free to be married . . . *[emphasis mine].*
>
> 1 CORINTHIANS 7:39

That verse clearly states that death frees us from the "bondage" of marriage, allowing the freedom of remarriage.

It is the term "bound" that interests us. Back in verse 15

• • •

we are told that the deserted Christian is *not* in bondage any longer. The normal sense of that term is clear. There is no need to seek some other sense. Being free of that "bondage" obviously means being free of the responsibility of that marriage. The desertion of the unsaved partner breaks the bond, thus freeing the believer to divorce and remarry.

Kenneth Wuest's *Expanded Translation* handles the thought quite capably:

> A *[Christian]* brother or *[Christian]* sister is not in the position of a slave, namely, bound to the unbelieving husband or unbelieving wife in an indissoluble union in cases such as these; but God has called us *[to live]* in peace.[2]

You probably don't need to be told that all sorts of suggestions have been made by sincere and qualified students of Scripture to explain what constitutes desertion . . . and to spell out what "not under bondage" really means. Because I promised to spare you numerous quotations and tedious pages of verbiage, I'll not attempt to represent all the opinions that range from unbelievably conservative to downright crazy (in my opinion!). But perhaps a word of caution is needed.

When we read of the departure of the unbelieving partner, obviously Paul is not referring to a temporary, quick decision to chuck it all and bail out . . . only to return in a little while. No, leaving means leaving. Permanence is definitely in mind. It implies a determined and willful decision that results in leaving the relationship with no desire to return, no interest in cultivating that home, no plan to bear the responsibilities, and no commitment to the vows once taken. That's "leav-

● ● ●

ing." And the one being left has little doubt in such cases. The marriage is over. Finished. Ended.

It was in just such a case I became involved many, many years ago. The wife and mother of three (a Christian) was literally "left" by her husband, who happened to be a medical doctor. The man, an unbeliever, would no longer tolerate her relationship to Jesus Christ, even though she was exceedingly careful not to cram it down his throat. In fact, she remained a charming, affectionate, and gracious mate in spite of his obnoxious actions and cruel remarks. Ultimately, however, he walked away. No provision was made to help her financially or otherwise. Embarrassed and heartsick, *his* parents stepped in and generously assisted their daughter-in-law for an extended period of time. Still . . . no word from her husband. He had definitely left. She remained faithful, but he was now gone.

A divorce followed. The woman walked with God through the whole painful experience. She was a remarkable model of patience and forgiveness. Bitterness never crept in. The marriage had ended, but by no means was her life finished.

Through a chain of events too lengthy to describe, she met the man who had been her high school sweetheart. He had never married, for in some strange way he was convinced the Lord would one day bring the two of them together. Although he had lost track of her whereabouts, he had this internal confidence they would someday marry. By the way, he was also a medical doctor . . . and had come to know Christ personally. Their courtship was beautiful to behold.

I had the privilege of officiating at the ceremony—an unforgettable delight. Just last year my wife and I saw them at a large Christian gathering. Their marriage is more solid

• • •

than ever. Both are spiritually on target. And their family, now grown, is a close, harmonious unit of deep and meaningful affection. Even though her unbelieving mate had left, God kept His hand on her life. He came to her rescue and met her need. In grace. In abundance.

## A Summary and a Warning

I agree with John R. W. Stott:

[Divorce was] *a divine concession to human weakness.*[3] No Christian should aggressively seek the dissolution of his or her marriage bond. Some of the very best things God has to teach His children are learned while working through marital difficulties. Endless stories could be told of how God honored the perseverance of abused and ignored partners as they refused to give up.

But in certain extreme cases, against the wishes and efforts of the committed mate, the marriage bond is destroyed beyond any human ability to restore it. Scripture teaches that God's "divine concession to human weakness" is occasionally justified, allowing the Christian divorced person the right and freedom to remarry in the Lord. There are three such cases set forth in God's Word, each provided by His grace:

• First, when the marriage and divorce occurred prior to salvation (2 Corinthians 5:17).

• Second, when one's mate is guilty of sexual immorality and is unwilling to repent and live faithfully with the marriage partner (Matthew 19:9).

• Third, when one of the mates is an unbeliever and willfully and permanently deserts the believing partner (1 Corinthians 7:15).

Before closing the chapter, a warning must be sounded. Being human and sinful and weak, we are all equipped with a

• • •

remarkable ability to rationalize. Unless we consciously guard against it, when we experience marital difficulties, we'll begin to search for a way *out* instead of a way *through*. Given sufficient time in the crucible, divorce will seem our only option, our long-awaited and much-deserved utopia. And we will begin to push in that direction, at times ignoring the inner voice of God's Spirit and at other times violating the written principles of God's Word. Either is a grievous act.

I warn all of us against such thought and actions. To carry out that carnal procedure is to short-circuit the better plan God has arranged for His people and, worse than that, is to twist the glorious grace of God into a guilt-relieving excuse for giving us what we have devised instead of accepting what He has designed.

Where God permits divorce and remarriage, humbly let us accept it without fear or guilt. Let us not call "unclean" what He now calls clean. But neither let us put words in His mouth and make Him say what He, in fact, has not said. No matter how miserable we may be.

There is something much worse than living with a mate in disharmony. It's living with God in disobedience.

## Notes

1. W. E. Vine, *Expository Dictionary of New Testament Words,* 4 vols. (Old Tappan, New Jersey: Fleming H. Revell Company, 1940), 3:109.

2. Kenneth S. Wuest, *The New Testament, An Expanded Translation* (Grand Rapids: William B. Eerdmans Publishing Company, 1961), p. 394.

3. John R. W. Stott, *Christian Counter-Culture* (Downers Grove, IL.: InterVarsity Press, 1978), p. 95.

• • •

# 10

# Commitment Is the Key

THE 1980 WINTER OLYMPICS ended yesterday. As I write these words, Monday-morning sports pages all across America contain similar headlines to the *Los Angeles Times*.[1]

## "THE AMERICAN DREAM TURNS TO GOLD"

A phenomenon has occurred. A bunch of no-name college kids and minor-league rejects have whipped the cream of international hockey—the Soviets, who had not lost an Olympic hockey game in *12 years* . . . who have been wearing gold medals since 1964!

No longer. A group of kids (all in their teens and early 20s) have startled the athletic world. Everyone except a coach named Herb Brooks and this gang of hot dogs on

• • •

skates said it couldn't be done. It was a silly, unattainable, impossible dream two weeks ago. Unlike the predictions of experts regarding speed skater Eric Heiden, who won five gold medals and emerged as the Olympic superstar, nobody gave this improbable little hockey team a second glance.

How did they do it? Honestly, now—what turned the American dream to gold? How was it possible for them to tie the Swedes, clobber the Czechs, beat the Russians, and come from behind to whip the Finns 4–2 for the final victory?

Well, if you are expecting a super-duper secret, you know, some hidden-surprise play they used, you obviously didn't watch the games. Those confident kids from the Midwest and East didn't rely on rabbit-in-the-hat tricks to win. They faced veteran finesse teams, one after another, with a game plan as old as hockey itself: Never back down, never quit, hang tough, keep hammering away, stay at it, regardless.

In a word: *commitment.*

In our permissive, irresponsible, escapism mentality, commitment is almost a dirty word. Those who would rather rationalize and run than stick with it and watch God pull off a miracle or two (not to mention shaping us in the process) resist this whole concept. If you, personally, are a runner, you are not going to like this chapter.

## A Vow Is a Vow

Marriage isn't begun in a context of vagueness and uncertainty. Two people, fully conscious and very much awake and aware, declare their vows. I realize vows may vary, but without exception, they include words like:

"... for better or for worse ..."

and

"... 'till death do us part."

● ● ●

Right? Remember those words you promised before God? Did He hear you? I'm being facetious—*of course He heard you!* Does He take such vows seriously? Read for yourself:

> When you make a vow to God, do not be late in pay-ing it, for He takes no delight in fools. Pay what you vow!
>
> ECCLESIASTES 5:4

Yes, He not only takes them seriously, He remembers them permanently. A vow is a vow. A solemn promise by which one individual binds himself/herself to an act or ser-vice or another person. What is it God commands?

"Pay what you vow!"

We are to fear God. He says so. We are to keep our word.

Now, listen very carefully. Read this slowly. No amount of psychological therapy, positive thinking (often dubbed "grace"), semantic footwork with the biblical text, alterna-tive concepts, or mutual support from family and friends can remove your responsibility to *keep your vow.* Unless you are a victim of the conditions I stated in the previous chapter (biblical bases for divorce and remarriage), you are responsi-ble for your marriage vow. I repeat—a vow is a vow.

Of course it's difficult! For sure, there will be times you are inwardly convinced you can't go on. But I remind you of your vow, your stated commitment:

"*. . . for better, for worse. . . .*"

What you are experiencing may be some of the "worse." And no marriage is exempt from such times.

The other day I drove over to some friends' house to pick up their daughter so she could go ice-skating with one of my children. The mom and dad were hanging wallpaper together.

•  •  •

Now . . . if you've ever done that as a husband-wife team, you know how tough that project is on a marriage. He and I laughed together as I shared with him the three stages couples go through when they hang wallpaper together:

First week: The couple considers separation.
Second week: The couple separates.
Third week: Divorce proceedings begin!

After the joke, he leaned over to me in the car and said something I wish I could hear every Christian husband and wife declare. With great sincerity, he stated these words:

"Chuck, do you know what makes our marriage work? One word: commitment. I am committed to that woman and she is to me—forever."

May his tribe increase.

## Why So Little Commitment?

What's happening? Why is the divorce rate skyrocketing? How come so many Christians are walking away from their commitment with no biblical justification?

I have boiled it down to four reasons. Perhaps there are many more, but these are the four I encounter most often.

*Public Opinion*   Ours is the "everybody's doin' it" craze. You know, the "don't sweat it" philosophy. The media ignores or, with a slick wave of the hand, glosses over the fact that a certain person recently walked away from his or her marriage. So does the press. If a person's books are doing well, who really wants to make waves about the author's private life?

All this dulls the senses of the public. The edge of our discernment is dulled. By and by we tend to tolerate (and later

● ● ●

*embrace*) the same compromise. No longer is it in vogue to be ashamed or embarrassed—certainly not to blush! Guilt is now an obscene term, something no one should bring on another by asking the hard questions. Public opinion okays actions—and thereby they stand approved.

This is nothing new. In Deuteronomy 6 God's people, the Hebrews, are just about to enter a vast, new territory. The promised land. Canaanite country. Sounds inviting, but it held numerous perils for those monotheistic, protected, sheltered people who had hovered around a cloud by day and a fire by night. Idolatry, humanism, and carnality in the raw awaited them in Canaan. And they would soon be living in that pagan culture where public opinion would be in conflict with their training under Moses. So God prepares them with this strong warning:

> "Then it shall come about when the Lord your God brings you into the land which He swore to your fathers, Abraham, Isaac and Jacob, to give you, great and splendid cities which you did not build, and houses full of all good things which you did not fill, and hewn cisterns which you did not dig, vineyards and olive trees which you did not plant, and you shall eat and be satisfied, then watch yourself, lest you forget the Lord who brought you from the land of Egypt, out of the house of slavery.
>
> "You shall fear only the Lord your God; and you shall worship Him, and swear by His name.
>
> "You shall not follow other gods, any of the gods of the peoples who surround you, for the Lord your God in the midst of you is a jealous God; . . ."

DEUTERONOMY 6:10–15a

• • •

Without question, the Lord God stood against His people being dulled and lulled to sleep by the people who surrounded them. How relevant! Public opinion has a way of weakening our commitment.

*Accommodating Theology*   There is another reason Christian marriages are weaker in commitment. I call it "accommodating theology." This is nothing more than fitting the Bible into my life style. In other words, I alter my theology instead of adjusting my life. My experiential tail wags the biblical dog.

Ezekiel the prophet faced a group of people who did this. Jehovah warned him ahead of time so it wouldn't jolt him too severely. Read Ezekiel 33:30–33:

> "But as for you, son of man, your fellow citizens who talk about you by the walls and in the doorways of the houses, speak to one another, each to his brother, saying, 'Come now, and hear what the message is which comes forth from the Lord.'
>
> "And they come to you as people come, and sit before you as My people, and hear your words, but they do not do them, for they do the lustful desires expressed by their mouth, and their heart goes after their gain.
>
> "And behold, you are to them like a sensual song by one who has a beautiful voice and plays well on an instrument; for they hear your words, but they do not practice them.
>
> "So when it comes to pass—as surely it will—then they will know that a prophet has been in their midst.

The Living Bible says it straight:

> "They hear what you say, but don't pay any attention to it" (v. 32b).

• • •

Now, don't misunderstand. They are not obnoxious and ugly. No. In fact, they are gracious, flattering, and even good at listening. But down underneath, they *really* have no plans whatsoever to let biblical theology get in their way.

This requires great rationalization. It demands the ability to ignore some obvious things, reinterpret and explain away certain passages of Scripture, and to call upon grace (that vast dumping ground for every conceivable act of disobedience) to get them through. By accommodating one's theology, it is remarkable what the mind can do to remove even the slightest trace of guilt! And by the way, it really helps to find an author or two to verify such accommodations.

I write with emotion. I'm sure it shows through. Within the past three years I have watched about ten marriages dissolve. All Christian marriages. Yes, both husbands and wives. All very much involved in Christian activities and church ministries. In each case one of the mates in each marriage has willfully (and skillfully) accommodated his or her theology so that the Scriptures actually "approved" their plans to walk out.

There were no ugly fights or bold public announcements like, "I am denying the faith!" No need for that. Calmly and with reserved respectability, they simply left. That's it. Against my counsel and strong efforts to stop them. Against scriptural injunctions. Against their mates' desires. In spite of the certain damage to their children. And regardless of the shame it brought against the name of God and the Church of Jesus Christ.

Hang on—not one seems to be wrestling with much guilt or personal shame. In fact, several say they have never been happier. A few openly insist they are closer to the Lord than

● ● ●

ever before in their lives. Some are still engaged in public ministries.

How? Accommodating theology, that's how. The enemy wins many a victory by this means.

***Delayed Consequences*** A third reason we see less commitment and an increasing number of broken marriages is a practical one—they get away with it without divine judgment.

Solomon once wrote about this:

> Because the sentence against an evil deed is not executed quickly, therefore the hearts of the sons of men among them are given fully to do evil.
>
> ECCLESIASTES 8:11

The Living Bible simplifies the verse:

> Because God does not punish sinners instantly, people feel it is safe to do wrong.

You've heard it before: "All God's accounts are not settled this month." I remember reading the words of a sixteenth-century saint similar to that one:

> "God does not pay at the end of every day. But at the end, He pays."[2]

I'll be honest. This is one of the most difficult things for me to accept. It's beyond me why a holy and just God does not deal more quickly with disobedience among His wayward children. It would certainly do a lot to build a wholesome fear in the lives of those being tempted to disobey. But even though I cannot explain it, I must declare it: Delayed consequences cause couples to walk away from each other.

● ● ●

Funny, isn't it? Being here-and-now thinkers, we tend to deny the devastating effects divorce will ultimately have on us and, for sure, on our children. Because momentary relief is such a determined pursuit by an unhappy mate, the added "benefit" of little or no divine discipline provides the encouragement needed to carry out the plan.

But the Bible clearly teaches that wrong will not ultimately win out. God never smiles on disobedience. At the end, let it be understood, He pays.

*Christian Approval*   There is a fourth reason so many believers are breaking the bond of marriage. It ties in with the third one we just considered. For lack of a better way to say it, Christian approval encourages it.

Remember the Corinthian church? Remember how lax they were with the brother in their midst who was living in sin? Listen to the account:

> It is actually reported that there is immorality among you, and immorality of such a kind as does not exist even among the Gentiles, that someone has his father's wife.
>
> And you have become arrogant, and have not mourned instead, in order that the one who had done this deed might be removed from your midst.
>
> For I, on my part, though absent in body but present in spirit, have already judged him who has so committed this, as though I were present.
>
> In the name of our Lord Jesus, when you are assembled, and I with you in spirit, with the power of our Lord Jesus,
>
> I have decided to deliver such a one to Satan for the destruction of his flesh, that his spirit may be saved in the day of the Lord Jesus.

• • •

> Your boasting is not good. Do you not know that a
> little leaven leavens the whole lump of dough?
> Clean out the old leaven, that you may be a new
> lump, just as you are in fact unleavened. For Christ our
> Passover also has been sacrificed.
>
> 1 CORINTHIANS 5:1–7

Church discipline is virtually unheard of in our day. The Corinthians were equally guilty of that same problem. They had a man who was guilty of incest. Rather than being ashamed, rather than applying discipline, they boasted about their tolerance and they were proud of how broadminded they had become.

And so it is in America today. Precious few are the churches that take a stand against disobedience in their midst. How seldom do we hear of someone being disciplined because he or she breaks his marital vow! Such Christian approval has helped foster a shallow view of commitment in our day.

## A Needed Clarification

It would be wise for us to pause a moment and clarify a matter seldom addressed in books on marriage, especially those that support commitment to the vows that were taken. There are unique occasions when it may be necessary for some couples to separate, temporarily. Due to various circumstances—all of them prompted either by emotional sickness or gross demonstrations of sin to the point of danger—there are times when life and health are seriously threatened. To remain together in such cases frequently leads to permanent damage and even tragedy in a home.

It is unrealistic and unfair to think that regardless of sure danger and possible loss of life, a godly mate and helpless children should subject themselves to brutality and other

● ● ●

forms of extreme mistreatment. *At that point, commitment to Christ supersedes all other principles in a home.* I am not advocating divorce . . . but I do suggest restraint and safety via a separation.

It is one thing to be in subjection. It is another thing entirely to become the brunt of indignity, physical assault, sexual perversion,  and uncontrolled rage. Since the believer's body is the temple of God's Spirit, it is *unthinkable* that He is pleased to have our bodies mauled and mistreated by sick and/or thoughtless mates who care little about their family's welfare and think of nothing but their own twisted gratification.

At such crisis times, call for help! Seek out a Christian friend who can assist you. Talk with your pastor or a competent counselor who will provide both biblical guidance and emotional support. And pray! Pray that your Lord will bring about changes in the unbearable circumstances surrounding you. Ask for deliverance, safety, stability, and great grace to see you through, to settle your fears, to calm your spirit so you can think and act responsibly.

What is it David writes?

> Be gracious, O God, for man has trampled upon me;
> Fighting all day long he oppresses me,
> My foes have trampled upon me all day long,
> For they are many who fight proudly against me.
> When I am afraid, I will put my trust in Thee.
> In God, whose word I praise,
> In God I have put my trust;
> I shall not be afraid. What can mere man do to me?
> All day long they distort my words;
> All their thoughts are against me for evil.

• • •

They attack, they lurk,
They watch my steps,
As they have waited to take my life. . . .
Then my enemies will turn back in the day
when I call;
This I know, that God is for me.
In God, whose word I praise,
In the Lord, whose word I praise,
In God I have put my trust, I shall not be afraid.
What can man do to me?

PSALM 56:1–6, 9–11

Powerful words, waiting to be claimed!

## Principles That Enhance Commitment

So far, much of what I have been writing has been more negative than positive. As I near the end of this chapter, I want to turn that emphasis in another direction. Let's consider several principles from 1 Corinthians 7 that enhance our marital commitment. To help make these thoughts stick, I will be brief and to the point. I find four principles in this great chapter.

*No Conflict Is Unsolvable*   1. Christian marriages have conflicts, but they are not beyond solution.

Take a look at 1 Corinthians 7:28:

But if you should marry, you have not sinned; and if a
virgin should marry, she has not sinned. Yet such will
have trouble in this life, and I am trying to spare you.

Writing with a compassionate heart, Paul says that he is trying to "spare us." One of his suggestions is that some not even marry (vv. 7, 26). But this is not God's will for most of

● ● ●

us. So then, when we marry, we can be sure of this—times of disagreement, fleshly flare-ups, are bound to happen.

*Remember this:* There is no such thing as a home completely without conflicts. The last couple to live "happily ever after" was Snow White and Prince Charming. Even though you are committed to your mate, there will still be times of tension, tears, struggle, disagreement, and impatience. Commitment doesn't erase our humanity! That's bad news, but it's realistic.

The good news is this: With the Lord Jesus Christ living within you and with His Book, the Bible, waiting to be called upon for counsel and advice, *no conflict is beyond solution.*

Before moving on to the next principle, drop down to verses 32 through 35:

> But I want you to be free from concern. One who is unmarried is concerned about the things of the Lord, how he may please the Lord;
> but one who is married is concerned about the things of the world, how he may please his wife,
> and his interests are divided. And the woman who is unmarried, and the virgin, is concerned about the things of the Lord, that she may be holy both in body and spirit; but one who is married is concerned about the things of the world, how she may please her husband.
> And this I say for your own benefit; not to put a restraint upon you, but to promote what is seemly, and to secure undistracted devotion to the Lord.

Talk about realism! If you are married, there is no such thing as giving the Lord your "undistracted devotion" 100 percent of the time. Know why? Because you married a *distraction!*

● ● ●

Just the difference between you and your mate—the male-female differences—have a way of keeping you trusting.

In our day of unisex and narrowing the gap between men and women, it is easy to pick up an erroneous idea that you and your partner are very much alike. No, that simply isn't true. Listen to one authority:

> An effort has been underway for the past few years to prove that men and women are identical, except for the ability to bear children. Radical feminists have vigorously (and foolishly) asserted that the only distinction between the sexes is culturally and environmentally produced. Nothing could be farther from the truth; males and females differ biochemically, anatomically, and emotionally. In truth, they are unique in every cell of their bodies, for men carry a different chromosomal pattern than women. There is also considerable evidence to indicate that the hypothalamic region, located just above the pituitary gland in the mid-brain, is "wired" very uniquely for each of the sexes. Thus, the hypothalamus (known as the seat of the emotions) provides women with a different psychological frame of reference than that of men. Further, female sexual desire tends to be somewhat cyclical, correlated with the menstrual calendar, whereas males are acyclical. These and other features account for the undeniable fact that masculine and feminine expressions of sexuality are far from identical. Failure to understand this uniqueness can produce a continual source of marital frustration and guilt.[3]

And never forget, those differences create conflicts . . . but in the Lord and under His control, none are unsolvable.

***Persistence Pays Off*** 2. Working through is harder than walking out, but it is God's way.

● ● ●

Again, listen to several verses from 1 Corinthians 7:

> Are you bound to a wife? Do not seek to be released. Are you released from a wife? Do not seek a wife (v. 27).
>
> Brethren, let each man remain with God in that condition in which he was called (v. 24).
>
> But to the married I give instructions, not I, but the Lord, that the wife should not leave her husband
>
> (but if she does leave, let her remain unmarried, or else be reconciled to her husband), and that the husband should not send his wife away.
>
> But to the rest I say, not the Lord, that if any brother has a wife who is an unbeliever, and she consents to live with him, let him not send her away.
>
> And a woman who has an unbelieving husband, and he consents to live with her, let her not send her husband away (vv. 10–13).

The obvious, underlying theme here is like our Olympic hockey team's game plan: Don't quit, hang tough, stay at it, regardless.

My wife and I declare our commitment to each other several times a year. We get alone, often for an overnight somewhere cozy and private. While there we look at each other and *verbalize* our promise to remain faithful. We actually declare aloud our commitment. Can't explain how or why it works, but there's something reassuring about putting things like that into words. As our ears hear what our mouths are saying (from our hearts, actually), our loyalty is reaffirmed.

Another fact is this: We have removed the term "divorce" from our vocabulary when we are working through a tough time. We do not refer to it, we do not use it as a threat, nor do we tuck it away in a safe place in our minds for some

● ● ●

future use. The passages we just read pulsate with commitment:

"Do not seek to be released. . . ."

". . . remain. . . ."

". . . the wife should not leave. . . ."

". . . the husband should not send his wife away."

Why? Why is it best to work through rather than walk out? I can think of several reasons:

• It is the continual counsel of Scripture.

• One's own growth in Christ is strengthened.

• The testimony of Christ before the public is enhanced.

• Working through forces needed changes. To walk out means we take our same hangups into the next relationship.

• Children in the family remain more secure, stable, and balanced. They also learn to run if parents run . . . or work out the difficulties if that's what Mom and Dad model.

I'm sure there are some who read these words and disagree—especially if you are thinking of walking out. Before you do, let me share with you a brief observation from an article out of a recently released secular magazine:

> No Role Models: For better or worse, divorce continues to split families at an alarming rate. The number of children involved in divorce has tripled in the last twenty years. And though parents, children and professionals are struggling to deal with such new domestic realities as single-parent families, there are no long-standing precedents, no established role models to draw from. Divorce and its aftermath can be a labyrinth of confusion and conflict, some of which may never be resolved.[4]

• • •

And then, quoting a professional divorce lecturer and author, Rabbi Earl Grollman, who believes divorce can be more traumatic than death,

> "The big difference is, death has closure, it's over. With divorce, it's never over."[5]

There can be no denying it. Walking out may *seem to be* the solution. Even the secular authorities are beginning to question that now. No, there is a better answer than walking out. Work through!

***God Defends Unselfish Commitment***   3. Being committed to one's mate is not a matter of *demanding* rights, but *releasing* rights.

Listen to these words:

> Let the husband fulfill his duty to his wife, and likewise also the wife to her husband.
> The wife does not have authority over her own body, but the husband does; and likewise also the husband does not have authority over his own body, but the wife does.
>
> 1 CORINTHIANS 7:3–4

A couple of words in those verses pierce deeply, don't they? Duty. Authority. Selfishness within us *hates* terms like that! "I've got my rights!" says today's liberated woman. "Hey, don't tie me down!" yells today's macho man. No marriage will flourish under that kind of philosophy.

God has a better way: Surrender your rights. Lay down your arms. Release your grip on the things you've been fighting for. Commit the risk to God. Trust Him to defend you and keep you from being ripped off. I say that to husbands

• • •

just as much as I do wives. Releasing rights, ideally, is a mutual thing—a duet, not a solo.

**Commitment Glorifies God** 4. The Christian's ultimate goal in life is not to be happy, but to glorify God.

This is one of the greatest insights God ever gave me. If you will meditate on it long enough, deeply enough, it will literally revolutionize your life. It has mine. It is based on the last two verses in 1 Corinthians 6 and leads into these thoughts we've been considering on commitment:

> Or do you not know that your body is a temple of the Holy Spirit who is in you, whom you have from God, and that you are not your own?
> For you have been bought with a price: therefore glorify God in your body (vv. 19–20).

Two significant thoughts deserve our full attention. I will personalize them:

I AM NOT MY OWN.
I AM TO GLORIFY GOD.

If it were possible to set in concrete one all-encompassing truth from this chapter, those two statements would do it. Please read them again.

Our ultimate goal, our highest calling in life is to glorify God—not to be happy. Let that sink in! Glorifying Him is our greatest pursuit. Not to get our way. Not to be comfortable. Not to find fulfillment. Not even to be loved or to be appreciated or to be taken care of. Now these *are* important, but they are not primary.

As I glorify Him, He sees to it that other essential needs are met . . . or my need for them diminishes. Believe me, this

• • •

concept will change your entire perspective on yourself, your life, and your marriage.

## A Concluding Thought on Commitment

We have thought about several reasons Christian marriages have grown weaker in our generation. We have also given consideration to some principles that strengthen our commitment to our mates. Every major point has been amplified from one or more biblical statements. And yet . . . I'm sure a few of you who read these words look upon your situation as an exception. Frowning, you'll lay this book aside with a sigh and think, "But you just don't know the person I'm married to. Our only answer is divorce. I just can't commit myself to this marriage. We're finished."

For your sake, I share the following letter. It was written to me almost a year after I spoke on commitment in our church in Fullerton, California. The wife who wrote it understands what a difficult marriage is all about. Believe me, I know. Their home seemed beyond repair.

Dear Pastor Chuck:

Tonight, I commented to you about how much I appreciated your comments concerning your stand on divorce, remarriage, and commitment. I thank you for your supportive and compassionate understanding of this area of difficulty in many marriages.

I really wanted to tell you how I have been blessed since I last wrote you nearly ten months ago (after you gave your sermons on commitment). I decided to remain steadfast in commitment to my own marriage that was in the middle of a divorce action at that time. God has changed me. He has given me a new love for my husband and, in turn, my husband has been changing in his atti-

• • •

tude toward me. He is still uncommitted about his relationship with Jesus—a miracle I am anticipating.

Six months ago we sat and listened to a psychologist (not a Christian) tell us to get on with the divorce because there was absolutely nothing left of our marriage and no basis upon which to build.

Well, God's grace has allowed the contrary. It's still a real struggle some days, but I have learned that as we "pull" toward each other rather than "push" at each other, the direction is more secure and sound. . . .

So, commitment is not just another word in my vocabulary. It has become a real part of my life.

In Him,
(signed)

No, commitment is not just another word. It is *the* watchword for a struggling, hurting, eroding marriage that seems destined to be locked up and closed forever.

Commitment is the key.

## Notes

1. *Los Angeles Times,* February 25, 1980, Part II, page 1.
2. Ann of Austria
3. Dr. James Dobson, *What Wives Wish Their Husbands Knew About Women* (Wheaton, Illinois: Tyndale House Publishers, Inc., 1975), p. 114.
4. Linda Bird Francke and others, "Children of Divorce," *Newsweek* [New York], February 11, 1980, pp. 58–63.
5. Ibid., p. 63.

● ● ●

# 11

...

# Don't Just Get Older, Get Better!

"Tomorrow we shall meet,
Death and I—
And he shall thrust his sword
Into one who is wide awake.

But in the meantime how grievous the memory
Of hours frittered away."

DAG HAMMARSKJOLD[1]

"Through his sorrow, Kunta was surprised to hear
that the old gardener had been called 'Josephus.' He
wondered what the gardener's true name had been—the
name of his African forefathers—and to what tribe they
had belonged. He wondered if the gardener himself had
known. Most likely he had died as he had lived—without
ever learning who he really was."

ALEX HALEY[2]

Growing older is a process from which we cannot escape.
As the reality of aging looms larger, strange things occur.

...

About the time we start making enough money to take care of our family's needs, the kids are grown and gone. About the time we have enough wisdom to pass on to the next generation, nobody cares to listen (except *grandkids*— God bless 'em!). And have you noticed how fast the years roll by? About the time your face clears up, your mind gets fuzzy!

And we've all seen the television commercial that shows a husband whispering tenderly into his wife's ear:

> "Honey, you're not getting older—you're getting better."

That's quite a compliment, even though it isn't true. *Everybody gets older.* Maybe we don't show our age and maybe we become sweeter with age. But, nevertheless, we do get older. And age brings tendencies that must be controlled. The real question that needs to be answered is: As we get older, how can we get better? Once all the children have left the nest and two people who honeymooned together 25 to 35 years ago are left to "start over," how can they find fulfillment and delight? How can they preserve that young-at-heart relationship during life's "afternoon" years?

There is an enormous resurgence of interest these days in restoring the grand old Victorian homes of yesteryear. In Los Angeles there is a large organization committed to such projects. Ninety-year-old dwellings that have "weathered decades of structural neglect and suffered the slings of deteriorating neighborhoods"[3] are now being handled with great care. Months are invested as skilled craftsmen and proud owners work hard (and spend multiple thousands) to renovate, refinish, restore, and preserve these elegant mansions of the past. As neglect and deterioration are arrested, beauty

● ● ●

returns. These places are not just getting older, they are getting better—literally!

## God Desires Our Restoration

An understanding and application of God's guidelines for restoring an aging marriage provide sufficient insurance to sustain the remodeled home when this critical time occurs. In the last two chapters of Ecclesiastes, Solomon sets forth several directives each couple must heed if they genuinely desire to "get better" as they grow older.

*Growing Old or Growing Up*   But first of all, we need to talk about the difference between "growing old" and "growing up." They aren't necessarily the same thing. Growing old requires nothing but living. Just the passing of time. Growing up requires a great deal of discipline.

To grow up, you must work on areas of your life that reflect irresponsibility, foolish thinking, and immature behavior. This is true whether you are 15 or 105! Growing old does not necessarily mean we have grown up. We may have to remind a child or teen-ager who's acting irresponsibly, "Grow up. Get with it. Act your age." At times we may need to say the same thing to ourselves, even though we may be in our 50s or 60s or 70s. Immaturity often rears its scowling head when couples realize their children are gone and for the first time since the honeymoon years, they're alone, together.

In his book *Homemade Happiness,* Wayne Dehoney puts his finger on this tender spot:

> When two parents wave good-bye to their last child, they are entering one of their most critical periods of marital adjustment. Two roads are open to them. They

• • •

may accept the situation as life's good gift to explore new heights of marital happiness. . . . Or they may travel a road in increasing loneliness, bitterness and neurotic behavior.[4]

Some people are surprised to learn that thousands of the couples who divorce each year have been married twenty years or more. This tells us that they have grown older, but many of them haven't grown better. They have chosen not to adapt, adjust, and work through this critical period of their marriage.

*Insuring Your Aging*   In this chapter, I want to sell you some insurance on your home. The premium has no dollar sign, but the price is terribly high. It requires that you grow up. The particulars of the policy are in Ecclesiastes 11 and 12. But we're going to look at the passage backwards—first Chapter 12, then Chapter 11. (Since I'm left-handed, going backwards makes good sense to me.)

In Chapter 12, Solomon has built to the ultimate climax. In unmistakable terms he clearly implies: "You're getting older." But in Chapter 11 he talks about how to live a better life, even though you're getting older. So, our study will go from the ultimate to how to prepare for the ultimate. Then, we'll find five guidelines for how to stay younger when you grow older.

## The Ultimate in Life: Old Age

Chapter 12 of Ecclesiastes is one of the most realistic passages in all the Bible. I love it for its picturesque symbolism and its sometimes humorous subtleties.

• • •

> Remember also your Creator in the days of your
> youth, before the evil days come and the years draw near
> when you will say, "I have no delight in them" (v. 1).

*Direct Warning* Notice that the chapter begins with a command: "Remember. . . ." An exclamation point could follow that first word. God wants you and me to remember *Him*. We are to remember the One who made us, and, ideally, remember Him while we are young, and throughout our growing-up years. (And these years never end, for we never become absolutely mature.) Why? Because there is that tendency in later years to look back and say we have no delight in them. Few people are more bitter and lonely today than those who have grown old alone, away from the Lord, and have turned against life. Verse 2 describes their gloom and depression:

> . . . before the sun, the light, the moon, and the stars
> are darkened, and clouds return after the rain.

Here in Southern California, we look toward the mountains after a rainstorm to enjoy the refreshing view. What a fabulous sight! Bright white mountain peaks stand tall as the sky is purged of pollution. But this isn't the picture here. Instead, there is an old person who, in bitterness, has closed himself in, and the clouds, instead of refreshment, bring only one dark storm after another.

Poet Joyce Kilmer wrote a nostalgic poem many years ago, entitled "The House with Nobody in It." The first and final sections tell the story:

> Whenever I walk to Suffern, along the Erie track
> I go by a poor old farm house with its shingles
> broken and black.

● ● ●

I suppose I've passed it a hundred times
But I always stop for a minute
And look at that house, the tragic house,
The house with nobody in it.

So whenever I go to Suffern,
Along the Erie track,
I never go by that empty house
Without stopping and looking back.
It hurts me to look at the crumbling roof
And the shutters falling apart,
For I can't help thinking the poor old house
Is a house with a broken heart.[5]

Sad and lonely as that scene may be, there is a tragedy worse than that. Much worse! It is the heartbreaking sight of a lonely, empty, crumbling life scarred by bitterness and cynicism. Solomon warns: Watch out! Keep the Lord in full focus!

**Old Age Unveiled**   And now the ancient king describes old age (v. 3):

In the day that the watchmen of the house tremble. . . .

That's describing the trembling lips of a person growing much older.

And the mighty men stoop. . . .

That's a picture of bent legs and a lower back stooped over in age.

The grinding ones stand idle because they are few. . . .

• • •

You have gums instead of teeth. Old age robs us of our ivories!

The other day when I was in a grocery store, I saw an older man dumping jars of baby food into his cart. I thought, "Wow, what a super grandfather. He is stocking up on that baby food so his grandkids will never go hungry." With a friendly grin, I walked up to him and said, "You're really taking care of the babies, aren't you?"

"What babies?" he mumbled. "These are mine!"

Grocers will tell you that older people often buy as much baby food as the young parents, simply because they can no longer chew. The problem? Their "grinding ones" are idle.

> Those who look through windows grow dim. . . .

The "windows" are your eyes. You know the facts: The older you get, the thicker the lens, the smaller the eyes behind it. I know all about that. I wear glasses with such thick lenses that when I get in a pulpit to preach, I have to be careful about looking at the spotlights, or my pupils might start smoking!

> The doors on the street are shut as the sound of the
> grinding mill is low. . . .

Deafness is setting in. You can't hear that grinding mill as well as you used to. Your pet phrase is, "How's that?"

> One will arise at the sound of the bird, and all the
> daughters of song will sing softly.

Insomnia. Here's an older couple who go to bed at 7:30 p.m. and can't understand why they can't sleep until 8:00 the next morning. At about 3 a.m. they wake up because the clock in the living room chimed three times. Light sleeping is part of

● ● ●

growing old. Funny, isn't it? Can't hear much during the day, yet everything at night is amplified!

> Furthermore, men are afraid of a high place and of
> terrors on the road.

Here's the problem of phobias. As we grow older we become afraid of high places, closed-in places, long journeys, or big crowds.

In my rebellious teen-age years, our family visited the capitol building in Austin, Texas. The capitol itself is built with a balcony that wraps around an open area. No matter what floor you go up on, you can lean over and see the Lone Star right in the middle of the floor on the first level. The higher you go, the more your stomach turns as you look over.

As Mother and I had just had an argument, my mouth wasn't doing what it should have been. When Mother looked over the balcony, she said, "Oh, it scares me to get this close. It makes me want to jump."

I answered, "Go ahead, I dare you!" Terrible thing to say! But when you get older and climb higher, you do begin to fear falling.

Youth knows no such fears. When I was a little kid, I often tiptoed across a fallen tree over a deep ravine below. That thing was at least twenty-five feet above the water. I remember tossing my sack lunch up in the air, catching it, and doing all sorts of crazy things out on that tree. I just have heart failure when I think about doing that now. Why? Because I'm now middle-aged. I'm no longer thirteen or fourteen. When I'm sixty, perhaps my fears will be even greater. Going on in the passage—

> The almond tree blossoms. . . .

• • •

Perhaps that's a picture of graying hair. At a distance an almond tree in full blossom has a snowy white appearance.

> The grasshopper drags himself along. . . .

His joints are stiff and perhaps he knows the crippling grip of arthritis. It's a picture of a wizened old man who can scarcely move those stiff limbs along.

> The caperberry is ineffective. . . .

Perhaps that would be sexual impotence . . . maybe the loss of appetite for food. Ultimately, in life, both occur.

> Remember Him before the silver cord is broken. . . .

Now it's serious. Here's a stroke which has broken the silver cord of life.

> Remember Him . . . before the golden bowl is crushed.

This is loss of memory. The golden bowl is probably a reference to our brain, which has housed so many facts in a lifetime. But in old age, we lose our memory. We forget names, places, and where we were. We lose orientation.

> The pitcher by the well is shattered and the wheel at
> the cistern is crushed.

Here are heart failure and circulatory problems. Then, in verse 7, he describes the ultimate:

> Then the dust will return to the earth as it was, and
> the spirit will return to God who gave it.

This passage has built to the climax of life—death.

● ● ●

*Saddle Oxfords and Varicose Veins* Ecclesiastes 12 reminds everyone who is growing older (but wants to grow better) that he or she should live realistically. The television commercial is a lie. Romantic as it may sound, you may *be* getting better, but you are *also* getting older. To deny that is to act out a fantasy. I don't know of anything more foolish than a 65-year-old man leaving his wife of some forty years to run around with a young chick who's barely twenty. He is trying to say, "I've still got it to together. I don't need that old woman. I'll go with this young one." It's foolish and yet it goes on all the time.

Even sillier is the aging grandmother who dresses like a high school cheerleader, knotty legs and all. Saddle oxfords and varicose veins don't mix. Old age has dignity and beauty until it tries to be a teen-ager. And nobody laughs over these archaic actors any louder than the teens. You've heard them: "Hey, get a load of that one. Look at her." Such people are not bridging the gap, they're *increasing* it.

The very best thing an older person can do is to admit, "I'm getting older. And I have something to offer just like I am." I appreciate this comment by one woman: "The happiest day of my life was when I stopped trying to look twenty years younger than I am and decided to be myself. There's a special beauty God has given my silver hair." That's the best compliment you can pay yourself. Just live with the fact that you are as old as you are. And ask God to keep you alive, charming, and "in touch."

By the way, your children will help you remember. One day I was in the car with our youngest daughter Colleen. She was singing a little ditty she learned at school:

> No matter how small a prune may be,
> He's always full of wrinkles.

• • •

No matter how small a prune may be,
He's always full of wrinkles.
A little prune is like his dad,
But he ain't wrinkled half as bad!
No matter how small a prune may be,
He's always full of wrinkles.

As we pulled in the driveway, she finished the chorus. She got out and slammed the door, looked at me and said, "Don't forget, Dad, I'm the little  prune. *You're* the dad." Off she skipped. I looked in the rear view mirror and thought, "Hey, she really ain't wrinkled half as bad." That's right. That's reality. Ugh!

*Support for What's Ahead*   The husband or wife who fears getting older and less attractive needs support from the other mate. Something tragic takes place in the heart of an individual who feels physical beauty is the only means for keeping a mate. That doesn't mean we should become ugly physically as we grow older. We need to do all we can do, and then stop and let nature take its course.

Facing reality will help prepare you for some of the danger signals of getting old and losing touch. Some of these are poor communication, loss of compatibility, and refusal to discuss and even compromise here and there. Mature people are not stubborn; yet some of the most stubborn people I know are in their sixties or seventies. They just haven't grown up. Mature people may have deep convictions, but they are open, tolerant, kind, and gracious. They have a long fuse, not a short one. Don't say, "That's just the way God made me." God wants to *remake* you. Your old nature makes you like you are. The new nature wants to remake you.

• • •

## Five Helpful Guidelines

Now, as we hang a close on this chapter, let's notice those guidelines I mentioned earlier. All but the first one are found in the previous chapter, Ecclesiastes 11.

*Face Reality*   The first guideline for growing old is *live realistically*. I've been talking about this all through the chapter: You're getting older. Now you should ask, "How can I get better? How can I grow up? How can I stay in touch?"

Those hard questions will assist you as you determine to be a realistic person.

*Enjoy Living by Giving*   The second guideline to help you get better as you grow older is *give generously*.

> Cast your bread on the surface of the waters, for you will find it after many days. Divide your portion to seven, or even to eight, for you do not know what misfortune may occur on the earth.
>
> ECCLESIASTES 11:1–2

Wise words from a wise man, written especially to those of us growing older. What is he saying? Listen to the paraphrase of *The Living Bible:*

> Give generously, for your gifts will return to you later.
> Divide your gifts among many, for in the days ahead,
> you yourself may need much help.

These two verses are telling those who have a little bit of this world's goods to share some of it and not keep it all to yourself. The happiest old people I know are those who give, and I mean give generously. Don't think that by keeping it

• • •

now you will enjoy it in the lives of your children later on after you're gone. Enjoy the results of it right now.

But I think the passage goes deeper than money. It includes money, but it's also saying, "Give of yourself. Stay in touch with the mainstream of life. Let the benchmark of your life be generosity. Let it flow. Let it go." It's when we pull back, close our doors, turn off our internal lights, and sit in selfish silence that we shrivel into the most miserable people on earth.

In connection with this, there's a danger when parents hesitate to release their older, unmarried children. They may be twenty-five, thirty, or forty, not married, and in a quandary over their relationship to their parents.

With my own family, I'm preparing for that right now. I was prompted by an excellent book by Charlie Shedd entitled *Promises to Peter*[6] to put down some goals I have for my children. Little by little, as they mature, I will release to them a certain level of leadership along with its responsibilities. I'll never call it back. By the time they have reached a certain level of maturity (not age, remember, *maturity* ), I'm going to put in writing their own, individual declaration of independence. I want to show them ultimately and officially that they are on their own.

Aside from a phone call, a handshake, or contact from time to time—which would thrill me to death—they're on their own to raise their lives before God. I'm there and I'm available, but I'm no longer their head.

Think about that. When you give *yourself* away, also give your children away so they're not left wondering, "Where do I stand?" Let them know they're on their own. Encourage them in it. It will help take away this so-called sorrow about

● ● ●

"losing your children." And you'll be gaining—and the world with you will gain—a responsible, purposeful citizen.

***Don't Plan for the Pasture*** The third reminder for growing older and better is *adapt willingly.* Read to verse 3:

> If the clouds are full, they pour out rain upon the earth; and whether a tree falls toward the south or toward the north, wherever the tree falls, there it lies.

Solomon is showing us the inevitabilities of life. Clouds will pour out rain, trees will fall. He then gives us a word of counsel:

> He who watches the wind will not sow and he who looks at the clouds will not reap (v. 4).

If the clouds come by, full of rain, it's going to rain. When the tree is cut down, it's going to fall and stay there. If you occupy yourself with the inevitables, the obvious, the ultimates, that's all you'll amount to—just an inevitable, obvious person who ultimately dies. You won't even sow and you certainly won't reap.

When you adapt willingly, you make plans to accomplish something. An older man who had just retired was asked by a young friend, "What are your plans, now that you're retiring?"

"Well, my first year I'm going to buy a rocking chair and put it on the front porch," sighed the older gentleman.

"Oh, that's great. What are you going to do the second year?"

"I'm going to rock in it."

Hey, listen to me! Sitting in a rocking chair and rocking away one's life is like watching the clouds rain and a tree fall.

• • •

All that stuff is obvious. Inevitable. It's not sowing and not reaping. When I think of retirement, I think, "Wow, that's your chance! You're free to put it all together!" You're unencumbered. God has given you enough time to really seek accomplishments—if you're ready and willing . . . to adapt.

Don't think older people are merely headed for the pasture. Four major poets who lived to be over eighty years of age did more work in the last decade of their lives than they did between ages twenty and thirty. William Gladstone took up a new language when he was seventy, and at eighty-three he became the Prime Minister of Great Britain—for the fourth time. At eighty-three! Alfred Lord Tennyson wrote *Crossing the Bar* when he was eighty. John Wesley was eighty-eight and still preaching daily with eminent success, eloquent power, and undiminished popularity. At eighty-eight! Every day! Michelangelo painted his world-famous *The Last Judgment* when he was sixty-six.

Had enough? Listen to these comments from J. Oswald Sanders as he writes about having a Caleb-like mentality:

> The late Canon C. H. Nash who founded the Melbourne Bible Institute and trained a thousand young men and women for Christian service, retired from his principalship at the age of seventy. At eighty, he received assurance from the Lord that a further fruitful ministry of ten years lay ahead of him. This assurance was abundantly fulfilled. During those years he was uniquely blessed in a ministry of Bible teaching to key groups of clergy and laymen—probably the most fruitful years of his life. When he was nearly ninety, the author found him completing the reading of volume six of Toynbee's monumental history as a mental exercise. . . .

• • •

> Mr. Benjamin Ririe retired as a missionary of the China Inland Mission when he reached the age of seventy. When he was 80 he decided to learn New Testament Greek. . . .

(Greek! When I tackled Greek, I was in my twenties and had my hands full!)

> . . . he became proficient in reading the Greek New Testament *[in his eighties!]*. At ninety, he attended a refresher course in New Testament Greek in a . . . seminary. When he was a hundred years old, he was present at a meeting at which the author was speaking. In his pocket was a small well-worn Greek lexicon which he used to brush up his Greek while travelling by public transport![7]

And to think that some people believe that retirement means "I'm finished." The Bible is full of illustrations of how those who are older are to teach the younger ones.

But in order to do that we *must* break out of any rut! Adapt willingly where you are right now. Old age is tough, but when you consider the alternative, it isn't *that* tough!

***Trust God: He Makes No Mistakes***   The fourth reminder is *trust fearlessly.*

> Just as you do not know the path of the wind and how bones are formed in the womb of the pregnant woman, so you do not know the activity of God who makes all things (v. 5).

You don't know the path of the wind and you don't know God's plan. So He says:

> Sow your seed in the morning, and do not be idle in the evening, for you do not know whether morning or

• • •

evening sowing will succeed, or whether both of them alike will be good (v. 6).

Here's a tender touch with reality. Solomon is saying, "Hitch your life to the only security there is, and that is the living, moving, active God." Nothing will keep a life younger than being in touch with the mainstream of God's activity. And that includes enduring loss as well as enjoying gain.

I appreciated what Catherine Marshall wrote following the death of her godly and dear husband, Peter. Prematurely stricken with a fatal heart attack (he was only forty-seven), Peter Marshall was shaping Congress and moving Washington D.C. as no man has done since then. Suddenly, he was gone. In describing how she overcame her grief, she said she finally became absolutely convinced that being lost in grief can become nothing more than a selfish act of self-pity. It's saying in effect, "I don't believe in a sovereign God. I don't accept the fact that He took my mate." When she realized that, she turned her efforts to writing. And who hasn't been blessed by Catherine Marshall's pen?

What is the alternative? To just sit alone and live alone? Solomon says, "Sow your seed in the morning and don't be idle in the evening." Like the old hymn says:

> Sowing in the morning, sowing seeds of kindness,
> Sowing in the noontide and the dewy eve;
> Waiting for the harvest, and the time of reaping,
> We shall come rejoicing, bringing in the sheaves.

Look at the second stanza:

> Sowing in the sunshine, sowing in the shadows,
> Fearing neither clouds nor winter's chilling breeze;
> By and by the harvest and the labor ended,
> We shall come rejoicing, bringing in the sheaves.[8]

• • •

Ever wonder what that meant? It means reaping the benefits of a fruitful life. Planting now, sowing now, being confident that God will raise it up later for something for His glory.

My grandfather is a living memory to me. That dear man was a household word in the little town where he lived and put in his strokes as judge and justice of the peace. L. O. Lundy was the byword for integrity. For some reason, God chose to take his dear wife, my mother's mother, at age sixty-three, much earlier than He took him. My granddaddy just took a notch in his belt and started in. One of the things he did was to build into my life. I'll never forget it. The times we were out fishing in the bay or the times in his home, he put his arm around me and just shared his life and the things he had learned. He just decided to pour it into me.

When my wife and I got married and we needed some financial help for our first home, guess who came to our aid? My granddaddy. I paid it back slowly but surely, and he never once reminded me of the debt. Faithfully, he stood by me. Little did he know the importance of the investment of his life in mine. He could have become a lonely recluse, locked himself in his huge home, and died early in self-pity. But he believed in a sovereign God who makes no mistakes.

I know a woman in Houston who once stood at her husband's grave, grieving. She suddenly realized, "There's no life here. Why are so many of us weeping over the tombstones." She determined before God, "This will be my ministry." She became a "cemetery evangelist," visiting with people who kept returning to that place trying to talk to the dead. Her vital faith in Christ led her to share Him with hundreds who grieved. That's her ministry. She may be getting older—but she's better than ever!

• • •

*You're Never Too Old to Rejoice*   There is one more princi-ple for growing old, in verse 7, *rejoice daily.*

> The light is pleasant, and it is good for the eyes to see
> the sun.

That means it is good to still be alive. It's good to be able to look up and see the sun, even though it may be blurred. Verse 8 adds:

> Indeed, if a man should live many years, let him
> rejoice in them all. . . .

There it is—rejoice daily! If you can't think of something to rejoice over, manufacture it. Ask God for it.

The other day I said to my wife, "Honey, I hope I never get too old to enjoy life."

She said, "You won't, honey, you won't."

The greatest delight of my life is just living—preaching, writing, laughing, studying, investing in my family's lives and in others' lives. It's a delight to stay young and be engaged in the lives of others.

The worst thing I could do—with all that I have gained through life—would be to carve out a cave and crawl into it, to wait until I die. There's too much going on outside to do that!

These guidelines will keep that from happening. Write them down and review them regularly:

Live realistically.
Give generously.
Adapt willingly.
Trust fearlessly.
Rejoice daily.

● ● ●

Take this prescription twice daily and, who knows, you may live to be a hundred.

And every year, you'll get better.

## Notes

1. Dag Hammarskjold, *Markings* (New York: Alfred A. Knopf, Inc., 1978), p. 6.

2. Alex Haley, *Roots* (Garden City, New York: Doubleday & Company, Inc., 1976), p. 357.

3. "The Reigning Victorians," in *Home* magazine, *Los Angeles Times,* 13 May 1979, pp. 14–20.

4. Wayne Dehoney, *Homemade Happiness,* J. Allen Petersen, ed. (Wheaton, Illinois: Tyndale House Publishers, 1971), p. 402.

5. "The House With Nobody in It" by Joyce Kilmer, copyright 1914 by George H. Doran Company from the book *Poems, Letters and Essays.* Reprinted by permission of Doubleday & Company, Inc.

6. Charlie W. Shedd, *Promises to Peter* (Waco, Texas: Word Books, 1970), pp. 21–31.

7. J. Oswald Sanders, *Robust in Faith* (Chicago: Moody Press, 1965), pp. 87–88.

8. Knowles Shaw, "Bringing In the Sheaves," *Triumphant Service Songs* (Chicago: The Rodeheaver Company, 1934), p. 139.

● ● ●

# 12
...

# What to Do with an Empty Nest

OF ALL GOD'S CREATURES on earth, humans have the toughest time with an empty nest. Mama bears seem to have no struggle at all saying good-bye to their cubs then going on their merry way. Dogs suffer no depression as their pups bound away to make their homes elsewhere. The same is true for horses with their colts, rabbits with their bunnies, and eagles with their eaglets. But humans? That's another story entirely.

## Five Stages in a Marriage

Marriages pass through progressive cycles, each one having its own unique set of challenges. Lofton Hudson suggests there are five distinct stages:

1. Family founding. From the wedding until the first child is born.

...

2. Childbearing. From the birth of the first child until the first child enters school.

3. Child rearing. From the first child entering school until that child begins college and/or leaves home.

4. Child launching. From the time the first child leaves until the last child leaves.

5. Empty nest. When the parents are alone until the death of one of the mates.[1]

It's the fifth stage I want us to think about briefly in this chapter. For sure, there are pressures and demands connected with the first four stages—sometimes making it almost too difficult to continue. There are, however, many more other subtle hazards that threaten a marriage as the nest empties.

## Some Empty-Nest Adjustment

It doesn't take great brilliance to name the problems of this stage in a marriage. Let me suggest several.

*Decreasing Physical Attractiveness*  Physically, we begin to show our age. We start to sag and slump! Erma Bombeck said it best when she admitted, "I've got everything I had twenty-five years ago. But now it's all four inches lower."

This plays psychological havoc with a marriage in these years. It affects our self-esteem, our sexual drive, our compatibility, and our feeling of oneness with our mate.

*Increasing Selfishness*  Hard as it is for us to admit, the empty nest is often occupied by two very stubborn, self-willed people. Chronic nagging and criticism can increase. Indifference toward people and life in general also tends to grow as does irritation in accepting the unpleasant and the

• • •

inconvenient in life. Few, indeed, are the older couples who happily adapt to the changes that impact their lives.

*Boredom and Depression*   Because of a number of factors, an empty nest can turn into a grim existence: unemployment, retirement with little money and no plans, sickness, fears, and the death of dreams in life. Who hasn't ached over aged parents who become trapped in this boring, depressing syndrome!

My own father lost the joy and light of his life when my mother died in 1971. She had been his spark, his motivation for living. Not being a "people person," he leaned on her for those delightful evenings with friends, those musical interludes each week, those fun times of conversation, laughter, trips, and visits with others. Her sudden departure left him stunned. Immobilized. Alone, in the truest sense of the word. Although we, his children, later cared for him and reached out to him, he soon became a man of boredom and occasional depression—a sad tragedy that often brought us to tears.

*Loneliness*   I did not mention this with the previous group because loneliness is, perhaps, the single most commonly mentioned difficulty of an empty nest. It needs to be considered by itself.

Busy, active children are gone. Car pools, ball games, piano recitals, school stuff, and everything from going on a date to selecting a mate are past. And rare is the marriage that stays healthy as it endures the vacuum created by all those things screeching to a halt. This is *especially* so if the husband-wife relationship needs the parent-child relationship(s) to keep it strong. Or if one of the parents found more

• • •

fulfillment in one of the children than in the marriage partner.

Another factor in loneliness we dare not overlook is widowhood. The pain of death is frequently increased because the living mate is left with only a small insurance policy and a mortgaged home. The kids are married and gone, friends and relatives are busy, and life quietly caves in, bringing that uninvited guest to every meal—loneliness.

*Retirement*   Although I mentioned this earlier, retirement brings its own unique adjustments that deserve special mention.

Retirement can be delightful or devastating . . . a dream come true or a dreadful nightmare. It all depends on how one prepares for it. If it "just happens," watch out! Many a marriage partner puts everything in neutral and rapidly loses touch with life. Like the attitude in a little poem you may have read:

> I get up each morning, dust off my wits,
> Pick up the paper and read the obits.
> If my name is missing, I know I'm not dead,
> So I eat a good breakfast and go back to bed.[2]

Right now that sounds like a super schedule to me! But I cannot imagine living like that on a regular basis with my wife and keeping our marriage strong. No, retirement often reveals just how much creativity we have . . . or how *little*. Being workaholics by nature, many American couples would be blown away if retirement suddenly occurred.

*Divorce*   A growing group of people in today's generation is the large body of divorced individuals. They live with anoth-

• • •

er kind of empty nest—an absent mate. This adds to the frustration of rearing children—a demanding job even for partners! Single parents struggle with very distinct experiences unlike those in any other type of family.

In recent years our church in Fullerton finally decided to ignore the single parents in our fellowship no longer. Under the very wise and capable leadership of one of my associates, Ken Bemis, we formed an organization called Single Parents Fellowship. I figured we may have fifty or sixty, maximum . . . but I was wrong. We have *hundreds* who now meet together on a regular basis. For worship. In small groups. To pray. To love and support one another. To share their anguish and struggles as well as their joys and pleasures.

It's booming! The benefits for having such a ministry far outweigh the difficulties. I would encourage other churches to do the same. Believe me, the divorced people in churches today are usually the loneliest, most misunderstood, most-often overlooked people in the flock.

These are just a few of the challenges that accompany the empty nest. Now let's turn our attention to some biblical counsel on what to do, how to cope—and even *enjoy*—the afternoon years of a marriage.

## Solomon Speaks Again

Remember the Scripture we dug into so deeply at the beginning of this book? Can you recall the section out of Solomon's writings in Proverbs? In case you have forgotten it was Proverbs 24:3–4:

> By wisdom a house is built,
> And by understanding it is established;
> And by knowledge the rooms are filled
> With all precious and pleasant riches.

● ● ●

Remember that famous "Swindoll amplified paraphrase"? It went something like this:

> By means of wisdom (that is, the skill of seeing things with discernment) a house can be remodeled into a home that attains to a flourishing condition—
>
> By means of understanding (that is, the ability to be sensitive and keenly aware, responding positively to others) that home can be set in order . . . made right—
>
> And by means of knowledge (that is, a teachable spirit that allows room for true facts to emerge) each individual area will overflow with valuable, worthwhile treasures (like memories and relationships) which will endure anything that comes.

With that in mind as our goal, let me share with you some closing thoughts on what to do as you see your nest emptying or, perhaps, as you stand *today* surrounded by the reality of an absent mate or grown children who have left the nest. I promise to be concise and clear.

## Three Practical Suggestions

Drawing these thoughts from the Proverbs passage, let's emphasize the three major terms by way of application.

*Exercise Wisdom* We learned that wisdom really means seeing with discernment. Like God does. Having *His* perspective. Looking on life as *He* looks on it. Such perspective will bring an enormous load of encouragement and objectivity.

But how? You're asking that in your mind, aren't you? Well, start by renewing your devotion to the Lord. If you are the superdependent type, you have been (in days past) all wrapped up in your mate or your kids. Almost totally. Losing one or both has thrown you into an emotional and spir-

• • •

itual tailspin. Small wonder you have become increasingly more lonely and immersed in self-pity.

Look up! Set a watch upon your heart. Begin meeting with the Lord at a particular time each day. That's right, *daily.* Get your Bible off the shelf and get back into it! Establish those vertical priorities that lead to a godly mentality. Refuse to let your feelings dominate and paralyze you.

One further thought: As you cultivate prayer, ask the Father for some specific assistance in keeping a divine viewpoint rather than strictly a human one. Ask for things like:

- Being freed from worry and fear (name some)
- The release of *your* will as opposed to His
- Ability to flex, accept, change, and shift
- Removal of self-pity
- Some ideas on how to be useful to others
- A healthy, active sense of humor
- Proper response to disappointments and loss

Seeing life with divine discernment is not a natural thing, it's *super*natural. But it is attainable, according to James 1:5:

> But if any of you lacks wisdom, let him ask of God,
> who gives to all men generously and without reproach,
> and it will be given to him.

And it brings such rich fruit. Read James 3:17:

> But the wisdom from above is first pure, then peace-
> able, gentle, reasonable, full of mercy and good fruits,
> unwavering, without hypocrisy.

***Employ Understanding*** Looking on life through God's lenses will arouse within you an enlarged capacity for sensitivity. Rather than just getting older, you will begin to see and think

● ● ●

deeper, respond better, and react sooner (and much more positively) to circumstances.

Wisdom leads to understanding. Let it happen! Since the empty nest stage usually provides you with more time, take advantage of it. You can become a person of such sensitivity, others will desire your presence. But in order for that to happen, you'll need to have the same prayer on your lips as this one:

> "Lord, thou knowest better than I know that
> I am growing older, will some day be old,
> Keep me from getting talkative, and particularly from the fatal habit of thinking I must say something on every subject and every occasion.
>
> Release me from craving to try to straighten out everybody's affairs.
>
> Make me thoughtful, but not moody, helpful but not bossy. With my vast store of wisdom it seems a pity not to use it all, but thou knowest, Lord, that I want a few friends at the end of life.
>
> Keep my mind free from the recital of endless details, give me wings to get to the point.
>
> Seal my lips on my aches and pains. They are increasing and my love of rehearsing them is becoming sweeter as the years go by.
>
> I ask for grace enough to listen to the tales of others' pains. Help me endure them patiently.
>
> Teach me the glorious lesson that occasionally it is possible that I may be mistaken.
>
> Keep me reasonably sweet; I do not want to be a saint; some are hard to live with, but a sour old person is one of the crowning works of the devil.
>
> Help me to exact all possible fun out of life.
>
> There are so many funny things around us and I don't want to miss any of them."[3]

ANONYMOUS

• • •

You see, understanding includes accepting and admitting our own tendencies yet trusting God to make us bigger, better people.

*Apply Knowledge*  Since God promises that the "rooms" of our marriage and home will be filled with valuable riches by means of knowledge, we need to take Him at His Word. As we learned earlier, the knowledge God honors and uses is *applied* knowledge. That kind is best demonstrated in a teachable, open, and nondefensive spirit. The kind that is always learning, forever reaching, probing, and discovering.

One of the most winsome traits to be found among older couples is this desire to learn and then apply that knowledge.

I teach the Bible. That's my bag. As a result I often find myself with my Bible open in front of congregations (none is better than the Fullerton flock!) as well as other groups. Periodically, I encounter couples who have reared their children and emptied the nest . . . and they somehow get hooked on learning the Scriptures. *Talk about fun!* I don't know who enjoys it more, they or I. And the best part of it all is that they genuinely care about putting into use what they discover in God's Word. And by the way, those couples seem to stay perpetually young. It's magnetic!

Well, that's it. Plain and simple . . . one, two, three. Easy to remember, and it works!

Exercise wisdom.

Employ understanding.

Apply knowledge.

In our fine church here in California, we have a delightful older couple whose lives have been anything but easy. Both have lost former mates by death and neither has known an easy life. Had they chosen to focus on their past, they could

● ● ●

certainly have shriveled up into narrow-minded, bitter, critical victims of self-pity. But they didn't. No way.

They found each other through a beautiful chain of events. They fell in love and decided to marry. It was marvelous! He was seventy-three, and she was seventy. You have never met two more involved, alive, alert, and positive people their age. Cynthia and I have been in their home on several occasions for dinner (with a roomful of others every time) and had the time of our lives. Their guestbook is half full of names before many months of any new year have passed. A steady flow of people is encouraged and ministered to because Klon and Christine Matthews refused to think, "We're finished. Our lives are over and done with." They are still on the cutting edge of life. I'm convinced neither one will ever stop until death finally overtakes them. They are an incredible pair!

That's the way to handle an empty nest. That's the way it is when God is given full freedom to step in, rebuild, and renew a drab house into a delightful home. He can do it and He *will* do it—empty nest and all.

## Notes

1. J. Allan Petersen, ed., *The Marriage Affair* (Wheaton, Illinois: Tyndale House Publishers, 1971), p. 401.

2. Ibid., p. 416.

3. Ibid., p. 420.

• • •

# 13
· · ·

# *Conclusion*

WO THINGS HAVE OCCURRED since I started this book months ago. First, I have aged several years. *Whew!* It's one thing to think, "I believe I'll write a book on marriage" . . . and it's another thing entirely to get the thing finished and into the hands of the publisher. I smiled recently when I read Jim Dobson's words as he quoted Sir Winston Churchill's comments on writing a book:

> Writing a book is an adventure. To begin with, it is a toy and an amusement. Then it becomes a mistress, then it becomes a master, then it becomes a tyrant. The last phase is that just as you are about to be reconciled to your servitude, you kill the monster and fling him about to the public.[1]

I certainly can identify with that!

· · ·

Second, our home has returned to a place of calmness and beauty. The remodeling process is just about complete. The drywall dust is gone. The plumbing is done. The tile is installed. The painting is complete. The carpet and flooring are in. The workmen have left. And I am sitting in a study surrounded by lovely oak bookshelves, brown-and-blue wall-paper, plenty of light. Outside the window is a winding brick walkway that is now finished. The front yard is still a mess, however. When the rains end we'll tackle that job. There are still a few places needing attention (there always *will* be), but for the most part, the place I call home now looks like it. The original design is now a beautiful reality.

God knew I needed a real, live illustration of just how much work is involved in remodeling. I thought it would be bad. But bad isn't the word for it. It was horrible!

But it's over. Praises be, it's over! I ask myself as I walk from room to room and as I write the last check to the contractor, "Was it worth it?" While I was in the middle of the mess, believe me, I would have paid somebody to take this place off my hands. But no longer. I'm glad we stuck it out. Yes, it was worth it all.

There's an old proverb Cynthia and I now understand and appreciate more than ever.

> Desire accomplished is sweet to the soul.

What we've endured in our house, you may be enduring in your marriage. Some of you are at the hardest part. You'd do anything to get out. You'd happily pay someone to take the thing off your hands. For whatever it's worth, don't. Please don't. God will honor your commitment as you determine to stick it out . . . to work through it. Take it from me, looking back in the years to come, you will be glad you did.

• • •

I can think of only one project that has been more difficult than remodeling our home . . . and that has been the remodeling of our marriage. I am honest when I say that of the two, getting a marriage together is far more uncomfortable, more costly, more time-consuming, and more demanding than getting a house in shape.

But it is also much more rewarding. The "sweetness of the soul" that comes from God's rekindling and preserving a marriage cannot be compared to any other accomplishment on the face of the earth. But unless the project is undertaken, something that was once beautiful and delightful will face and fail.

Some time ago a very talented young lady wrote a poem at my request. I told her about this book I was writing and then asked that she create on paper the scene of marriage in need of attention. Perhaps her words describe where you are coming from.

I especially appreciated what she wrote because she described something she had had to imagine in her head. She is not married—yet. She will be, however. She is my future daughter-in-law, Deborah Jean Morris. I'm convinced you will read more of her work in the years to come:

> In those days
> the words, "I love you, honey,"
> were said with fifty different inflections
> and meant fifty different things.
>
> They could have meant
> thank you for opening the catsup bottle,
> even though you said that I had loosened it first.

• • •

Or I enjoy our talks
when you come home from work
and there's just the two of us to share and dream.

Or simply that I appreciate all those things
that make up you;
your sensitive strength,
the way you smile me off my soapbox,
or the way that you pretend you are listening
when you read the paper.

But somewhere along the way we turned
and instead of floating with the current,
we now struggle against it.

It wasn't one action, or one word,
but a series of little unresolved spats and quarrels
that now make the TV the solution
to the problems of a hard day
and silences us when we should say
"Thank you" or "You really look nice today."

Today, I no longer tell you that I love you
because the sound of those words
mocks the special meaning that they carried
when we were first wed,
and it is too painful to remember
that those feelings we said we would never lose
were, tear by tear, left in the past.[2]

How true. How terribly true! Not just one action or one word. Not a single little isolated incident once or twice a year . . . not huge chunks pulling loose, causing sudden devastation. No, not that. But rather a subtle, almost unnoticed wearing away . . . a series of little yet consistent cracks, ever

• • •

widening and silently ignored. It happens every day of every year all around this globe of hurting humanity. It is a universal problem in marriages . . . *but it is not inevitable.*

And that is why I have written this book.

I long to communicate to every couple I can possibly reach that the living Lord has designed a way to make it work. He holds out hope and encouragement—a divine blueprint for marital restoration. And because He is the Originator of the plans, I can declare (without reservation) they are workable, reliable, believable, and attainable. And best of all, He promises His strong arms of support and assistance to all who determine to return to His inerrant Word and trust Him through the painful yet essential process of change.

Are you willing?

Will you trust Him in spite of your seemingly impossible situation?

Please do! He anxiously awaits this opportunity to strike the original match in *your* marriage as you allow Him the room He needs to rekindle and preserve the flame that once was there.

### Notes

1. Dr. James Dobson, *What Wives Wish Their Husbands Knew About Women* (Wheaton, Illinois: Tyndale House Publishers, Inc., 1975), p. 177.

2. Deborah Jean Morris (unpublished poem, March 2, 1980).

• • •

# Discussion Guide

# Introduction to Discussion Guide

THE AMERICAN FAMILY is in trouble. One authority on marriage has said that our society has reached the point where happily married couples seem to be an "oddity." Even though some form of the family has been found in every known society, one anthropologist has now demanded a substitute for the family unit. Frederick Engles, most widely known as one of the creators of modern communism, made a similar demand over a century ago. It has been estimated that some 20 million American couples live in desperate unhappiness and unfulfillment. The number increases every year.

This sad scene has also affected Christian marriages. And there is a desperate need to right this devastating trend with the power and knowledge that God has made available.

We need to get back to the basics. Who designed the home

• • •

anyway? Since God brought forth this human relationship, what does He consider to be essential in marriage? How has He planned for marriage not only to survive, but also to be genuinely fulfilling and satisfying?

## The Aim

The aim of this discussion guide is to explore the ground that has been broken in this book. It is designed to enable every couple to discuss and answer those questions in the preceding paragraph. This guide will also help a group of couples gather together to talk about the essentials of marriage, and then relate how marriage can survive and even thrive in today's society—all from a biblical perspective.

## What's in the Guide?

The discussion guide will aid the leader who invites a group of couples to study this book together. The guide has twelve studies to coordinate with the twelve main chapters of this book. Each assignment is divided into four areas. There is a section on the purposes of the assignment, a section expressly devoted to the study of Scripture, a section labeled *Thought Questions,* which are exactly that, and a final section called *Putting It into Practice,* which will help a couple apply the study to their lives.

A *Scripture Index* and a *Subject Index* are also provided in the back of the book to help those who wish to dig deeper and research the scriptures mentioned in the book. The *Scripture Index* gives a listing of every verse that is used and the page on which it is used. Use the *Subject Index* to quickly locate the author's view on key issues and topics.

• • •

## Where Do We Meet?

Ideally, this can be a three-month study for a group of interested couples. It would be preferable for the gathering to be a once-a-week affair in a non-threatening setting such as the home. At least six people are needed to reduce the tenseness that probably crops up in a small group, but as many as eight couples can participate effectively. Just remember—the larger the group the more readily the information can be gathered, but the less deeply the issues can be pursued.

## Who Should We Invite?

The big question about one of these fellowship gatherings is always, "Who do we invite?" If you want a group composed of married couples, ask people with common interests, who are about the same age. Or, as a pastor, you may wish to gather engaged couples together in a group fashion with this study as the focus. A pastor might even want to gather couples together who need marriage counseling. Possibly a study could be made up of engaged couples formed out of a college fellowship group. Whether couples are about ready to get married or about ready to celebrate 25 years of married life, this study can be used effectively to rekindle and build that marriage flame!

## What Is Expected of Us?

In approaching the assignments in the discussion guide, a person should remember that the assignment schedule is coordinated with the chapters in this book. The designated book chapter needs to be read before tackling the discussion guide. Then a couple needs to read through the *Purposes* section in the guide, and individually (or together) work

• • •

through the *Scripture Input.* The *Thought Questions* apply to families as well as couples, so take time at the dinner table to discuss one thought question per day. Make an effort to implement the action step as it applies to the couples' group or your home, or both! When you return to the study each week, you'll have plenty of questions, reports, and suggestions to discuss and share.

## How Do We Begin?

Getting started is an exciting time in such a group study. When you talk to couples about participation in the study, ask them to be willing to invest the time for the study and the money for the book. Commitment at the front end of the study is always best. And if couples will agree to this, you can purchase the books and have them available at the first meeting. That is much better than having staggered purchases of the materials throughout the life of the small-group project.

Explain the purpose of the study at the first meeting. Show the couples the format of the discussion guide, and how that format should be followed at home as well as in the weekly discussion study. Be sure to maintain this format at each weekly meeting. You will experience a strong temptation to jump to the final section and share how the week went with the spouse and family. Don't yield to that urge! Go through the *Purposes,* the *Scripture Input,* and the *Thought Questions* first. In the end you will be pleased you stayed with this methodical game plan. So will those in the group.

Time is crucial in a study such as this. Plan for at least one hour of unhindered interaction time with the discussion guide material. You may want to plan and enjoy about a half

● ● ●

hour of refreshments and "milling" before you start your group discussion. This is especially true for the first session. Concerning time for each of the assignments, the leader should ask for about two hours of discussing and reading outside the weekly session time. That's only about 3% of a couple's available time in a week after work, rest, and meals. And your marriage is certainly worthy of the investment!

## Anything to Be Careful of?

A few comments need to be made about personality tendencies of individuals that can hinder the progress of the group. Occasionally, there is the attitude of domination—the "Bull Moose" tendency of controlling the discussion either for the sake of flattery or because of a "know-it-all" complex. Another destructive attitude as far as possible group interaction goes is that of playfulness—a little light-heartedness certainly helps to break the ice in any situation, but continual side-tracking by "Mr. Tom Foolery" through jokes and puns about every statement can only prove distracting and irritating. On the other side of the scale, the "Sad Sack" approach that comes from the "it-will-never-work" pessimist or the easily offended pouter is equally destructive to group progress. Finally, the seemingly unharmful approach of "standing in the wings" or looking on without comment is not healthy in a group discussion.

It would be good to talk about these unhelpful attitudes graciously and honesty at the first study. Frankly, all of us have one or more of these tendencies. As you discuss these attitudes, talk about ways to (1) encourage participation by all the group, (2) stay on the subject at hand, (3) allow and appreciate times of silence by the group for thought, (4) create an atmosphere where couples are free to share and free to

• • •

fail, and (5) guard against embarrassing anyone for any reason.

One more thing. In most groups there will probably be the need for a baby-sitter. Why not talk about getting one or two people to be sitters for the entire group of children? Share the expense between couples. Then, when the 12-week study is over, honor the person or persons who have served you in this way. Sponsor one couple from your group to treat the person(s) who did the babysitting to a special evening.

Enough of rules and guidelines. Let's dig in and see what God has to say about marriage!

And before plunging in—why not pray? Pray specifically that God will make each study meaningful and encouraging.

• • •

# 1

. . .

# *Let's Consult the Architect*

## Purposes

To get a good look at the original marriage.

To be made aware of 4 steps that we can take in our own marriage to make it strong.

To examine the 3 essential qualities you will need as a couple in order to make the 4 steps work.

## Scripture Input

Read Genesis 1:12, 18, 21, and 31, 2:18–25; Psalm 127:1; Proverbs 2:6, 24:3–4.

1. In comparing the verse in Genesis 2:18 with the verses of Genesis 1:12, 18, 21, and 31, you will note that a list of positive statements is counteracted by a negative statement. What was God's reason for saying, ". . . it is *not* good"?

2. How did God remedy Adam's "isolation" problem in Genesis 2:18? What do the words "a helper suitable for

. . .

him" mean from a husband's perspective? From a wife's perspective? Be specific.

3. They say that a dog is a man's best friend. What does Genesis 2:19–20 say about that statement? Discuss the unique meaning of the words "a helper suitable for him."

4. Look at Genesis 2:21–25. How did the creation of woman differ from the creation of other animal life? God didn't create woman from dust as He did man, either. Does that say anything to you about the uniqueness of woman?

5. What does Adam's reaction in verse 23 (in *The Living Bible*) tell you about the Designer's foresight of Adam's explicit needs in a wife? Do you share in this thought about your husband or wife? Why or why not?

6. Adam was whipped into shape from dust. Eve's physical structure was formed from bone and sinew—Adam's bone and sinew. Is the difference in origin significant? Since you and your mate have differences in make-up and attitudes, does this passage say anything to you? List the differences you do have—everything from personality to tastes, from talents to eating habits. Talk through the importance of these differences to your marriage.

7. What 4 guidelines for a meaningful marriage are found in Genesis 2:24–25? These will be discussed in the next chapter, but stop and talk about these principles now. Using each portion of Scripture like ". . . a man shall leave his father and mother" as a guide, paraphrase the 4 principles in your own words.

8. Look closely at the words of Proverbs 24:3–4:

> By wisdom a house is "built,"
> And by understanding it is "established";
> And by knowledge the rooms are "filled"
> With all precious and pleasant riches.

• • •

Concentrate on the actions suggested by the verbs. Now note the objects of these action verbs. What do these verbs suggest as the primary "construction" activity of any couple who own their own home?

9. Look up the following verses in relation to the topics, Wisdom, Understanding and Knowledge—Proverbs 1:5–7, 2:1–11, 3:13–26, 4:4–12, 7:2–4, 8:1–12, 9:1–12, 10:13–14, 13:14–16, 16:21–24, 19:8, 22:17–21. What are the differences in meaning of these 3 terms? How do these qualities apply to your marriage and home? Are they being hindered in their use at your house? If so, how?

10. Read Psalm 127 together. Discuss ways these words are becoming a reality in your home. Try to be specific.

## Thought Questions

11. Imagine for a moment that God did not bring you "a suitable helper." How would this affect your life today? Discuss the differences it would make in your family if the helper had been "unsuitable."

12. Using Genesis 2:21–23 as a basis for discussion, share with your partner and your family the unique qualities you see in him or her. Let each family member add to the list. Take these responses and use them as short "thankfuls" during table blessings this week. (Be careful! Some of the positive statements that leak out from these meetings could startle your neighbors!)

13. Make a list of all the things that you value in your home, from stereos to workshops, from sewing machines to picture frames. If your house was destroyed, what "valuables" would remain from your home? Think honestly: "How much emphasis do I place on *things* in our home?"

• • •

## Putting It into Practice

Discuss the essentials of the perfect home from a biblical viewpoint. Construct a "group exchange" where ideas from each group member are noted on a blackboard or overhead transparency. Act and react about how reforms or reinforcements can bring about needed changes in your imperfect home. On your own as a couple, try hard to affirm your love for one another as you deal honestly with the reality of things as they are in your home.

• • •

# 2

...

*Let's Repair the Foundation*

## Purposes

To delve into the 4 marriage-strengthening principles of Severance, Permanence, Unity, and Intimacy.

## Scripture Input

Read Genesis 2:24–25, 3:9–10; Matthew 19:4–6; 1 Corinthians 7:3–4; and Ephesians 5:22–23.

1. Read the account of the actor's response to the question "What makes a great lover?" Share your initial feelings about his statements in light of current popular opinion about alternatives and "temporariness" in marriages today. What does the Bible say on this subject?

2. Meditate on the following clause:

> "For this cause a man shall leave his father and his mother . . ."

...

What is the context—that is, the biblical words and sentences surrounding the verses—of this statement? Does marriage signify a "break from the past"? In what ways? Read Ephesians 6:1–3 and discuss how the principles of severance and respect of parents can be retained when two people leave their families and establish a new home.

3. Think about severance from the perspective of a parent. How can a parent help to effect this principle? How can a parent hinder the home-leaving process?

4. Add on the next part of this verse:

> "For this cause a man shall leave his father and his mother, and shall cleave to his wife . . ."

As you think about the verb *cleave,* remember that it means to "cling," or "adhere to." Keep this in mind as you look at the following passages:

2 Kings 5:27—leprosy "clings" to one's body

Job 19:20—bones "cling" to skin (in the case of an emaciated, diseased person)

Jeremiah 13:11—a waistband or belt "clings" to the waist of a man (in order to tightly restrain or hold firmly out of the way a person's tunic so that free movement is allowed)

The sensation you should get from studying this verb is that a tight, close, firm-holding action is being described. Apply this to the marriage bond. What does it say about a man's and woman's marriage union? What does it indicate about God's view of this bond?

5. Jesus referred back to this main passage on marriage (Genesis 2:24–25) when questioned by an intimidating group of religionists about divorce. Read Matthew 19:4–5 slowly. Now look at Jesus's statement in verse 6, especially the last clause. What was Christ's view of the permanence of

● ● ●

marriage? According to Christ, who actually consummates the union? Does this give you a new view as to why a breaking of this permanent bond is so unbiblical? Explain your answer.

6. Study the next phrase of Genesis 2:24.

". . . and they shall become one flesh."

We are looking at the principle of *unity* here. Do the words "shall become" indicate a process or an instantaneous fact? What advantage is there in seeing marriage as a continuing series of steps toward a goal rather than a "once and for all" accomplishment at the altar? Has anyone reading this guide ever "arrived" as far as marriage is concerned? Briefly discuss a couple or three processes you are currently working through.

7. There are some telling words recorded in 1 Corinthians 7:3–4 about unity in marriage. Verse 4 states that a husband has full authority and freedom over his wife's body in respect to marital affairs. Verse 4 also states that a wife has full authority or freedom over her husband's body in the same way. How can this be accomplished? What personality tendencies could get in the way of such an unselfish arrangement? Is this type of unity described elsewhere in the Bible?

8. Intimacy is a delicate subject. Genesis 2:25 is a biblical description of tender intimacy in marriage. Honor and beauty describes the marriage bed rather than shame and disgust. Obtain a copy of *The Living Bible.* As husband and wife, read the account of the Song of Solomon to one another, the husband reading the part of King Solomon and the wife reading the part of the woman. What does this biblical book teach you about openness and intimacy in marriage? (For a more descriptive and elaborate study of this biblical book,

● ● ●

read Craig Glickman's *A Song for Lovers,* an InterVarsity Press publication.)

## Thought Questions

9. A good exercise that tests your family's spiritual barometer is to take Ephesians 5:15–21 and talk about it at the dinner table. Are these things true in your family unit? Is there harmony, gratitude, and humility being demonstrated between family members?

10. Hold a family "panel discussion" and talk about the *severance* principle. Discuss the pros and cons of leaving the "nest" too quickly or not quickly enough. Now, switch roles in the discussion, the parents representing the side of the children and the children the parents' role. Make plans for this future event in your family's life. Talk about how that process can begin now and continue for several years.

11. Think about your commitment to each other, as family members and as spouses. How long has it been since you have *verbally* declared that to one another? Is it time to have an "eyeball-to-eyeball" commitment talk with one of the family members . . . alone with each other and in a place you won't be interrupted?

## Putting It into Practice

Using the 4 guidelines of Severance, Permanence, Unity, and Intimacy as measurements of marital success, take a poll of marriage partners at the office, store, shop, etc., to see which of these principles have been put into practice. Take stock of your own marriage. Does the absence of any one of these necessitate certain repair measures in your own home? When can these repairs start taking place?

● ● ●

# 3

• • •

*Bricks That Build a Marriage*

## Purposes

To discover and put to use the practical building materials for healthy marriages that are found in the Bible.

## Scripture Input

Read aloud Proverbs 31:10–31; Ephesians 5:22–23; 1 Timothy 3:4–5; and 1 Peter 3:1–9.

1. We will refer to Ephesians 5:22–23 again in this study. Place it in front of you in several different translations if possible. What is the extended comparison that is used in this analogy? God is described as the bridegroom and His people as His bride elsewhere in the Bible. Read Ezekiel 16:8–14 for the analogy of God as the bridegroom and the people of Israel as the bride. What is significant about these comparisons? Do they say anything to you about God's concept of marriage?

• • •

2. God thinks highly of the relationship called marriage. In fact, He thinks so much of marriage that He compares the husband-wife relationship to the relationship of Christ to the church. As you think about the church's relationship to Christ, wives, what attitudes are most important for the church to demonstrate to her Savior? Does this carry over into your marriage? What attitudes did Christ display toward the church, husbands? Is this being demonstrated in your marriage?

3. Carefully construct the biblical definition of submission. Take your time. Choose your wording wisely. Is this understood in today's culture? Define sacrificial love according to Ephesians 5:25. Do most Christian husbands you know show an understanding of this concept? Why or why not?

4. Read 1 Peter 3:1–2. What is the "belief-instilling" instrument God uses on a husband from the life of a submissive wife? How can a woman's actions be the most powerful evangelism tool in a home?

5. A contrast is set up between verses 3 and 4 of Peter's third chapter. Two types of adornment are described—inner and outer. Does this section dictate dark, morbid attire for all godly women? Or does it suggest a doormat type of attitude for women who aspire to have imperishable qualities God deems precious?

6. A gentle and quiet woman, that is, one who has a dignified self-control and a tranquil attitude that radiates confidence and assurance, is described in Proverbs 31:10–31. Is this picture of a godly woman familiar to you? If not, read about her in this passage of Scripture. Look for similar situations in your home's life style that would allow for such a display of virtue.

• • •

7. "Thus Sarah *obeyed* Abraham . . ." This same verb is used in Hebrews 5:9. What is the result there?

8. In 1 Peter 3:6, the wife's response of obedience brings forth belief in the husband's life, too. How do you feel about the response of obedience, wives? Is there an assurance that you won't be exploited for your submissive response? Where? But what about that wife you know who is being taken advantage of by her husband?

9. Passivity in male leadership has diseased Christian homes everywhere. Yet church leadership demands good home managers for its office holders (cf. 1 Timothy 3:4–5). In what ways does 1 Peter 3:7 address this subject?

10. Patient understanding is a virtue of the godly husband according to 1 Peter 3:7. Think specifically of the times *this* week you have neglected to sit down with your wife after work and listen to her day's problems. What took the time she really deserves?

11. A wife is called a "fellow heir" of God's grace. Strong words! What do they mean? Is there any penalty for not giving this honor to your wife, husbands?

12. As a couple, employ the 4 suggestions given at the end of Chapter 3. Be ready to share the results at the weekly group meeting.

## Thought Questions

13. Can you think of a woman in your past who literally fulfilled the 1 Peter 3 role of a wife? How did she affect those around her, especially her husband? How did she affect you?

14. Do the same as you did in question 1 in thinking about Peter's conception of a husband. Husbands, share unguarded reactions and feelings about such a model for a male. (If you think this person only exists in superman story-

• • •

books, say so! But be ready to listen to examples of men who are actually filling this role—empowered by the Holy Spirit.)

15. Meditate on 1 Peter 3:8–9 as a family. Think of family situations where these qualities do or don't exist. Then talk about bringing them into reality. Deal specifically with each quality, one by one.

## Putting It into Practice

Each day this week, read Ephesians 5:22–23 to one another—first the wife's portion (5:22–24, 33b) and then the husband's (5:25–33a). Each time reference is made to a wife or husband, insert your own first name. Ask God to make these attitudes real in your actions toward your mate this week. Pray with one another, asking God to assist you in accomplishing this desire.

• • •

# 4

. . .

# Watch Out for Cheap Substitutes!

## Purposes

To be made aware of the inferior building materials some couples settle for as they hammer out their own marriage design in place of God's.

## Scripture Input

Read Genesis 27 and 1 Peter 3:1–9.

1. "What you see is what you don't get!"

That should be the label on much of the synthetic and artificial merchandise that is peddled in stores as a replacement for the real thing. From flowers to fabrics, the purpose is to fool. Talk about some of the synthetics and substitutes that are found in every store. List what imitations can and cannot do. Now apply these thoughts to the use of cheap substitutes in marriage rather than genuine qualities of godly character.

. . .

NOTE: In these next questions, you will be using Scripture as the source of the positive actions for marital success while examining the substitutes that some couples use.

2. As you read 1 Peter 3:1–2, underline the words *won without a word*. Secret manipulation (winning another over by unfair means) is cited as a substitute used by some wives to win their way. God says win by behavior—man says master by manipulation. Think about some common manipulative techniques. Turn to Proverbs 3:3–8. What are the benefits of truthful, straightforward dealing? What are the advantages of doing things God's way?

3. A clear biblical example for secret manipulation by a wife is found in Genesis 27. Read about Rebekah's secret maneuvering with her favorite son, Jacob. Are there lessons to be learned from this story? (Not only was there animosity between Esau's people, the Edomites, and Jacob's people, the Israelites, during the remainder of biblical history, but Jacob was the victim of deceit and scheming in Chapter 29—proof positive that deceit breeds deceit!) Be honest, now. Can you recall an occasion when you used manipulation to get what you wanted?

4. Type out the words of 1 Peter 3:3–4 on an index card, and tape it to the mirror in your bathroom. This exercise is to remind you of the danger of concentrating too much attention on external beauty. Consider the time you spend in front of the mirror each day. Is there too much time being spent here daily? What inner-beauty preparations could use some of that overtime in front of the mirror? Can you name an inner-beauty trait you really need to develop?

5. There is an emphasis on "doing" what is right in 1 Peter 3:6. Ladies, list the major activities that you do each

• • •

week. How many of these activities relate to your husbands and families? Do you need to reevaluate your schedule?

6. Again our passage is 1 Peter 3:7. The substitute that masquerades as the breadwinner complex takes hold of many a husband after marriage newness wears off. Read 1 Corinthians 13:4–7 aloud and slowly. List the number of times providing a living is listed as a characteristic of Christlike love. Is there more to love than insurance policies? Name some specific ways your love could be better demonstrated.

7. The wife is described as the "weaker vessel" in this section of Scripture. This distinction of weakness can be appreciated by comparing your finest china to your rugged cast-iron skillets. Hence, delicate fragility rather than inferior quality is being stressed. Think about that. Are there advantages in understanding your wife's "weaknesses"? Are her physical limitations appreciated at your house or is she put under pressure because of them?

8. Intimidation is a tactic used by some husbands to manage their wife and family. What are some examples of intimidation? What light does 1 Peter 3:7 shed on this subject?

9. Another unbiblical attitude for the husband who uses substitutes is the tendency towards smothering instead of honoring "as a fellow heir of the grace of life." Look up Galatians 3:28, a verse that refers to every Christian's standing before Christ. Although the roles of man and woman are different in a marriage, what is the same as far as one's relationship to Christ? Do certain leadership styles of Christian husbands deny this reality? How? What part does uncontrolled jealously play in the use of this substitute? What is the cure for domination or smothering? How could a change be effected?

● ● ●

10. First Peter 3:8–9 sums up the attitudes that combat cheap substitutism.

> "To sum up, let all be harmonious, sympathetic, brotherly, kindhearted, and humble in spirit; not returning evil for evil, or insult for insult, but giving a blessing instead; for you were called for the very purpose that you might inherit a blessing."

Now take these verses, and do the following exercise. Turn all the positive statements into negative ones. For example, write "let all be *un*harmonious, . . . returning insult for insult," etc.

Before you exclaim how horrible this twisted version is, look at your own home. Honestly, does your home resemble this type of selfish behavior more often than not? On a scale of 1 to 10 (1 being most of the time and 10 being very rarely), rate your marriage and family life as to how often the biblical version of 1 Peter 3:8–9 is a reality. What specific steps could you take to improve this rating? Are you willing to trust God to bring about these changes, painful though they may be? Pray seriously about *one* major factor that currently hinders the change. Ask Him to remove it.

## Thought Questions

11. Review the 3 substitutes wives often use to cover up what's missing in their marriage. Contrast these with the 4 bricks of Chapter 3 that wives are advised to use. As a wife, how do you feel about your building in these areas? As a husband, how do you feel about your spouse in this regard?

12. Review the husband's substitutes and the real bricks he should be using. As a husband, how do you measure up? As a wife, how do you feel about your spouse?

● ● ●

## Putting It into Practice

Take some time to think about your goals as a couple. What can you change as a wife, as a husband, to make those goals come true? What substitutes need to be replaced in your marriage? Have a blab session in your group this week. Brainstorm and come up with concrete steps that can be taken to eliminate the cheap substitutes from your marriages and achieve the biblical goals you have as a couple.

• • •

# 5

...

# Who Says the Honeymoon Must End?

**Purposes**

To explore the ways in which a couple can develop a fulfilling, mutual intimate relationship so that meaningful romance and sexual desire will never lose its edge.

**Scripture Input**

Read Genesis 1:27–31; Proverbs 5:1–15, 15–21; Song of Solomon 5:10–15, 7:1–10; 1 Corinthians 7:1–5; Hebrews 13:4.

1. What are some of the common misconceptions about honeymoons? (For example, that there are no differences of opinion during this time, that sex is always an enjoyable experience right from the start, etc.)

2. Are there advantages to seeing the honeymoon as an adjustment period rather than a romantic dream with no flaw? Would this have helped you before marriage? Were there some "honeymoon hangups" that have seriously impacted your sexual relationship today?

...

3. In conjunction with the reading of Genesis 1:27–31, note the declaration "it was very good." To what may this declaration be applied in the preceding verses? Does this statement apply to the command, "Be fruitful and multiply . . ." (vv. 22, 28). What, then, is *God's* opinion about sex?

4. Turning to the pages of the New Testament, we see that God's original blessing upon marital intimacy did not change.

> "Let marriage be held in honor among all, and let the marriage bed be undefiled . . ."
>
> HEBREWS 13:4

Literally, the first of that verse reads:

> "Marriage is honorable in all."

In order to get an idea of the "precious value" God attaches to the marriage relationship and all that goes with it— including sex—let's examine His use of that word "honorable." Look up the following verses: 1 Corinthians 3:12; James 5:7; 1 Peter 1:7, 19; 2 Peter 1:4; Revelation 17:4, 18:12, 16, 21:11, 19. Keep in mind that the word translated "precious, very costly" is the same word translated "honorable" in Hebrews 13:4.

What else does this adjective describe besides the marriage union? Does the fact that God places the same value on marriage that He does on priceless gems, the rich promises of the Word, and even the invaluable blood of His own Son affect your concept of marriage? Of marital intimacy?

5. Is sex only intended for procreation and propagation of the human species? Read Proverbs 5:15–19. Answer this question with more than a "yes" or "no."

6. Take a copy of *The Living Bible,* and read Song of Solomon 5:10–15 and 7:1–10. The first passage is a speech

• • •

about his wife. Does the presence of such passages in the Bible add to the emphasis that has been made about God's high view of sex? What can each spouse learn about display of affection within marriage from these verses? (Read 1:8–9, 2:3–6, 4:1–15, and 6:4–9 as well.) Is communication an important part of marital intimacy? Are you and your spouse free to communicate about these things?

7. Study 1 Corinthians 7:1–2. Is our society a believer of this principle?

8. What are the consequences of sex outside and prior to marriage? Some biblical passages that pertain to this subject include Proverbs 5:1–6, 6:20–35, and 7:1–27. Think about the "reversal of roles" mentioned in the fifth chapter of this book.

9. We have cited 1 Corinthians 7:2–3 as keystone verses for the principle of unselfish affection being a part of intimacy within marriage. Look up the following verses to build your backlog of truth about the principle of being unselfish: Romans 12:10; 1 Corinthians 10:24, 13:5; 2 Corinthians 5:15; Philippians 2:3–4; James 2:8.

10. Can a correlation be drawn between moral failures in Christian marriages and the lack of strong sexual relationships in those same marriages? What does 1 Corinthians 7:5 contribute to your thoughts here?

## Thought Questions

11. Think back to the honeymoon that you took as a couple after you were first married. What made it so special? What attitudes did you have that contributed to the enjoyment of those first days together? Which of those attitudes are still in operation today?

12. Take some of the passages from the Song of Solomon

● ● ●

that we studied and write them down on paper. From the wife's standpoint, what is appreciated about the husband's words to the wife? From the husband's standpoint, what does he appreciate about the wife's words to her husband? Verbalize some of your own creative compliments to your mate using this Scripture for a guide.

13. Some say marriage is a "50-50" proposition. What would happen, however, if each mate gave 100 percent to the other?

14. Think about Cliff Barrow's suggestion of maintaining marital harmony by the use of these 4 phrases: "I am wrong," "I am sorry," "Please forgive me," and "I love you." Would that solve a situation of disagreement you're facing with your mate today, and keep the honeymoon going?

## Putting It into Practice

Construct an imaginary interview in which a family member or discussion group member questions you during the first week of your marriage. Have the interviewer draw up a list of questions about your view of marriage during those first honeymooning days. Use this dramatization to spark a discussion about how your ideas of marriage have or have not changed.

*A Special Creative Project:* Want to try something *really* unique? Write a *very* intimate love note to your mate—much like the ones you read in Song of Solomon. Spell out your affection, the things you really adore about your partner. Don't be afraid to tell it like it is (Solomon wasn't!). For an added surprise, tuck it under his/her pillow . . . or mail it to him/her. But be sure and put *personal* on the envelope. Nothing like having one of your kids rip open that love letter and read it at the supper table!

• • •

# 6

...

*Termites
in Your
Troth*

## Purposes

To discuss the "little" problems that can weaken the marriage relationship from the inside like termites can weaken the foundation and internal structure of a house.

## Scripture Input

Read Song of Solomon 2:15 and Ephesians 5:15–21.

1. As you read Song of Solomon 2:15, replace the word "foxes" with "termites" and the word "vineyards" with "marriage." Can you think of any "little" things that are eating away at your marriage relationship?

2. Turn to Psalm 139:23, 24. Again, replace the words "hurtful way" with "termites." What admonition surfaces when you rephrase the verses in this manner? How does that relate to marriage?

3. Let's look closely at each of the termites spoken of in Chapter 6 of this book. The warning in Ephesians 5:15 is to "be careful how you walk." Don't be confused about your

...

role as a husband or wife. Can you recall the material we have studied that gives clear and unconfused input about our roles in marriage? (Here's a hint to help you remember—the biblical books of Genesis, Proverbs, Song of Solomon, 1 Corinthians, and Ephesians are noteworthy places to start.)

4. There are 3 sources of marital confusion cited in this book. The following befuddlers are cited: anti-marriage propaganda in our society, demands on parents' time and efforts because of the number of relationships in a family, and immaturity on the part of the parents. Match the following verses with the appropriate problem mentioned above: Colossians 3:12–14; Ephesians 5:15–16 and Galatians 6:2; Proverbs 2:6–15.

5. Another of the termites that infects the homebuilding process is the one labeled *busyness*. Doing too many things—even though they are good things—in the hours that each of us are allotted. It would be good to get God's perspective on the use of time. Turn to Psalm 90 and slowly meditate on the words. What new things did you learn about time? Who does the writer suggest we can turn to for direction in our time management? Why?

6. "Workaholic" is a descriptive term for the plight of many men and women today. Does God say that work is not good? Read Luke 10:7; Ephesians 4:28; 1 Thessalonians 4:11–12. But is work "for the sake of work alone" good? Before you answer that question, read the thoughts of a man who discussed the subject of work for the sake of work alone—Ecclesiastes 2:18–23. If you are a high-achiever, better read these words again.

7. There is a balance between work and rest, a balance which even the Son of God recognized in His ministry on earth. In Mark 6:7–12, the disciples were sent out in pairs to

● ● ●

minister. Upon their return, what did Jesus instruct them to do? Read Mark 6:30–32. What principles might we apply to our own lives from this?

8. The word "foolish" in Ephesians 5:17 can be interpreted to mean a lack of common-sense perception or a want of reason. The cure for a lack of common sense, the lack which can become an insensitivity to God and man (the third termite), is to know the will of the Lord. See what the following verses teach about the will of God: Romans 12:2, Ephesians 6:5, 6; Colossians 1:9, 10; 1 Thessalonians 4:3; Hebrews 13:21; 1 Peter 2:15. How can this knowledge counteract the third termite?

9. Stubbornness. Every red-blooded American has this characteristic to some degree. Mixed with a little rugged independence, it becomes some of the grit which forms the backbone of our country. But that same stick-to-your-guns attitude can become lethal in marriage. Meditate on this phrase:

> "be subject to one another in the fear of Christ."

What does that phrase tell us about an independent spirit in marriage?

10. The verb used in Ephesians 5:21 means to put oneself under the authority of another. When neither husband nor wife wants to give in during the heat of a disagreement, how would this verse apply? What is the motivation for yielding to the other spouse's authority according to this verse? What about mutual submission?

11. One result of persistent bullheadedness is recorded in Proverbs 29:1—a broken neck! What are other results that can be expected from a stubborn attitude that insists on its own way?

● ● ●

## Thought Questions

12. Review the 4 termites that work on the sly to destroy marriages. Think about each one as it relates to your half of the marriage. Are there individual corrections you can make to improve your marriage? How do you feel about them as your sole responsibility, not your partner's?

13. Think again about the word submission. In the past, has it only been applied to the women in the house? Has this study changed that wrong conclusion? Apply "submitting to one another" to several household duties or tasks. Husbands, don't dodge this one! Are there some things your wife has mentioned again and again that need your attention?

## Putting It into Practice

Make the following list of termites:

Confusion in the Home
Busyness that Runs Roughshod Over Others
Insensitive to Anyone but Self
Stubborn Attitudes that Don't Yield

Include this rating scale:

Yes—It is a problem for 1 or more family members
No—It is not a problem
Maybe—It someday could be a problem

Have family members apply it to your home. Where are the danger areas? What can be done to shore up these weaknesses? Once again, husbands—how about setting a date when you will follow through with your wife's requests? You will be amazed at how it affects her willingness to cooperate with you in some of your requests. Start soon!

● ● ●

# 7

...

# *How to Have a Good Fight*

## Purposes

To surface some reasons why disagreements occur in marriage and to discover how a couple can maintain a proper attitude during times of conflict.

## Scripture Input

1. Before you begin this section of questions about Scripture that relates to "good" fighting behavior, inventory your premarital understanding of one another. Did you know he liked TV sports? Did you know she liked to go to bed early and get up early? Did you know he was not handy with tools? Did you know she craves a clean house? Did you lead each other into thinking incorrectly about your likes and dislikes? Were you *really* honest?

Continue this probing of things you have discovered (or are yet to discover, if you aren't married) *since* the time that

...

you were married. Have you had disagreements over these postmarital discoveries? Did the "love is blind" syndrome blur your vision of these trouble spots? Have you admitted this to each other yet?

2. Honesty is the best policy. Ephesians 4:25 lays this truth on the line regarding our speech. Read Philippians 4:8. Notice the first 3 adjectives. Where does honesty begin? Will honest actions stem from honest thoughts? Paraphrase your own rule about thinking and speaking in honesty during disagreements.

3. Can you be angry without sinning? That is the meaning of Ephesians 4:26. This is anger under control. The same emotion was resident in Jesus at the time He cleansed the temple—notice Matthew 21:12–13. Talk about the ways that anger can be controlled in your disagreements.

4. What are some problems with out-of-control arguing? Relate Proverbs 18:14–19 to this situation. Are there some deep emotional scars your rage has caused in your marriage? Again, be honest.

5. A third rule for fighting involves timing. Ephesians 4:26–27 talks about the ceasing of arguments before they stretch to the next day. Read Ecclesiastes 3:1–8. Is there a time to engage in a dispute—rather than covering it over—and a time to refrain from debate? What are some times that are absolutely "out" in your marriage as far as heated discussions are concerned? What signals do you watch for in your mate which indicate that the time is inappropriate?

6. We have talked about honesty, proper control, and timing as rules for "good" fighting. Ephesians 4:28 gives us another. A negative command is followed by a positive encouragement. A similar use of words occurs in the next verse. In most cases, a negative prohibition in the Bible is fol-

• • •

lowed by a positive counteraction. Does this characterize your criticism of your mate? Can you give positive suggestions for those negative appraisals you make of his/her actions? Why are you more critical than encouraging? Tough question . . . but it needs to be addressed.

7. Tact is the watchword of the fifth rule for fighting. Do you know how to say the needed word without offending? Meditate on Proverbs 15:1, 2, and 4. Discuss the advantages of being tactful.

8. We are told to put away from us "all bitterness and wrath and anger and clamor and slander"—along with all *malice*. This word means a spiteful type of wickedness. When you combine bitterness through slander with malice, you've got a public defamation for sure. Is public criticism of your mate a problem for you? Do you often use sarcasm to cut him or her down? What is this verse saying to you?

9. Read Ephesians 4:32. Now look up Colossians 3:12–13. Write out a definition of forgiveness from these verses. Does Christ's forgiveness of you have any bearing on your attitude toward your mate after a fight?

10. What is the best way to stop a fight as suggested in Chapter 7? Can you remember a recent fight when admitting your wrong did not end the conflict? Or have you tried this solution yet?

### Thought Questions

11. Who is the winner in any heated fight? Can a fight occur without some scuffs and scrapes and cuts being inflicted on both contenders? Talk about this fact—that everyone's a loser in an unfair fight—in relation to your home struggles today. How can you disagree without assaulting your partner?

● ● ●

12. The tongue can inflict deadly wounds during fights, either by open destruction or cutting sarcasm. One way to combat the tongue's evil work is to eliminate the words "never" and "always" when referring to your mate's short-comings. For instance, don't say "she always does so and so" or "he never does this." Are these a couple of vocabulary words you two need to delete from your disagreement dialogues? How about the word "divorce"? If there are some terms that are "off limits," agree to their removal together. Both partners must cooperate.

13. Ephesians 4:30 speaks of the empowerment for all the character changes needed in your fighting patterns. What are the ways in which you grieve the Holy Spirit, prevent Him from enabling Christ's life to shine through you, when you ignore the fighting rules that have been outlined? Try to be painfully specific.

## Putting It into Practice

Role play each of the seven rules for fighting. First act out the wrong responses—not being honest, not using proper control, using poor timing, etc. Then act out the right responses properly observing the rules. Have different family members act in roles other than their own, reacting the way they see Mom, Dad, brother, or sister behave. Use the dramatizations as the basis for further discussion about family disagreements. Be ready to laugh. When you see yourself acted out in someone else's skin . . . it can be hilarious! And terribly convicting.

• • •

# 8

...

'Til Debt Do Us Part

## Purposes

To educate couples about one of the most common havoc-wreakers in a marriage—the mismanagement of money. And hopefully, to offer some guidelines for a couple who wants to manage their finances well.

## Scripture Input

Read Proverbs 11:1, 14:23, 15:27, 22:7, 23:4–5, 27:23–24; Ecclesiastes 5:10; Matthew 22:15–22; Luke 19:11–26; Romans 13:6–8; 2 Corinthians 9:6–8; 1 Timothy 6:8–10, 17–19. (Ever wonder why they say that the Lord has more to say about money than the topics of heaven and hell combined?)

1. Several wrong attitudes have been developed by Christians with regard to money. One of the first is that the money you put in the bank is yours, except for the tenth you set aside for God. What does Psalm 50:10–11 say about any material thing on the earth? Read Luke 19:11–13. The

• • •

nobleman in the parable is the Lord, and notice His attitude toward those He leaves His money with. Whose money is in the servants' possession?

2. A second wrong attitude is akin to the first. In Luke 19:13, the nobleman says "*Do business with this (money) until I come back.*" Should we distinguish between our business practices and the "Lord's work"? Should we operate with any less integrity at the office than we do in conducting church business? What does Colossians 3:23–24 say about whatever business practice in which you engage?

3. Verse 14 of Luke 19 shows the antagonistic attitude some citizens had toward their leader's input about their money affairs. Often, we would rather do business our way than God's way—it's more comfortable, using the habits we are accustomed to. Read Psalm 127:1 and James 4:13–17. Do each of these passages favor including God's leadership in business? Does this approach differ from yours?

4. Note the reaction of the master to the profits made by his servants in Luke 19:16–18. Rather than seeing the making of profits through wise money handling as unspiritual, what does the master's reaction indicate about God's attitude toward wise stewardship? Look up 1 Corinthians 4:2, Titus 1:7, and 1 Peter 4:10. Is wise stewardship a debit or a credit on God's ledger? What's another reason for keeping current on the wise use of your money according to Luke 12:42–48?

5. Some people believe God smiles on self-imposed poverty. The stories of Luke 19:19–22 and Matthew 25:24–30 should forever dispel that notion. After reading those sections of Scripture, talk about your neglect of wise stewardship that has been due to the belief: "Having a little is more spiritual than having much." How much of that attitude is the result of just plain laziness?

• • •

6. Discipline is a requirement for any wise steward. Even the discipline to put money into savings is cited as more worthy than dumping it into a checking account according to Luke 19:23. Let's take a lesson on discipline from our friends the ants, here. Read Proverbs 6:6–8. Now that's using foresight and discipline! Should discipline be incorporated into your money affairs? In what ways?

7. Some say the rich get richer and the poor get poorer. How does Luke 19:24–26 qualify that statement?

8. Study the figure in Chapter 8 which details the peaks and valleys of earning. How many years do you have left to plan your investments? Have your children been informed—if they are old enough—of your plans? Have you shared wise management principles with them? Are you working with them in practical ways so they are putting these principles to work right now?

9. As you read Matthew 22:15–21, spell out the implications of Jesus' quick statements. Are you as purposeful in your giving to God as you are in your giving to government? Mentally compare the way you prepare your taxes and the way you determine your year's giving to the Lord. Which do you spend more time with? Which contribution will go further—eternally?

10. In Romans 13:8, the admonition is given to not be continually in debt to someone else. See if the following verses contain advice for your credit buying: Nehemiah 5:1–5; Proverbs 22:26; Matthew 18:25. This may hurt: Are you abusing your use of credit buying? Why?

11. A proper perspective on use of money is given in 1 Timothy 6:8–10, 17–19. Is money in and of itself evil? If the proper attitude toward money is maintained, what avenues of service open up to those with wealth? Look up

● ● ●

Acts 20:35. Compare this well-known quote with 1 Timothy 6:17–19.

## Thought Questions

12. Think about the four suggested guidelines for financial planning: Christ and Ceasar are essential, not optional; buying and borrowing demand short accounts; savings and security require planning; things and treasures are temporal. Translate each principle into a current family project. Engage your family in those projects.

13. Look at the suggested "10-70-20" plan included in Chapter 8. Calculate your budget—taking taxes and tithes first—according to this formula. How do you come out on the scale? Any plans to start some needed changes?

## Putting It into Practice

Debate each of the seven attitudes below in your home or couples' study. Have one pro voice and one con voice. (1) That part is God's . . . this part is mine. (2) God isn't concerned with secular things. (3) Let's not get fanatical! Leave God at church. (4) Success is suspect . . . profit-making is unspiritual. (5) Having little is more spiritual than having much. (6) Ignorance is bliss. Someday our ship will come in. (7) God isn't fair. The rich get richer and the poor get poorer.

Talk with your mate about struggles you've had with one or more of these attitudes. If it's necessary, seek the forgiveness of your partner for your failure with money management. If your partner has been disciplined and wise (occasionally without your support), *thank* your mate for being a consistent model.

• • •

# 9

...

# Divorce: When It All Comes Tumbling Down

## Purposes

To understand and pursue solutions for the one problem that mars God's original blueprint for marriage—divorce.

## Scripture Input

Read Genesis 5:1–3; Psalm 103:10–12; Matthew 19:3–9; 1 Corinthians 7:12–15, 39; 2 Corinthians 5:17; Ephesians 2:1–7, 19–27.

1. The picture of the original marriage was one of sinless happiness. But with the first sinful act of disobedience that was performed, what happened to the marriage that had been open before God? Read Genesis 3:1–15. How did this affect future marriages, as well as the state of man and woman individually? Compare Genesis 5:1–3 and Romans 5:12. How does the encroachment of sin affect man's attitude toward divorce? Matthew 19:8 will help you determine the answer.

• • •

2. Before we go further with biblical teaching on divorce, let's lay the groundwork for understanding what a marriage is. What actually constitutes a marriage?

   a. consent of the 2 partners
   b. leaving the respective homes
   c. a ceremony
   d. sexual intercourse
   e. any of the above
   f. all of the above
   g. none of the above

3. Look up the following verses as they relate to a marriage union: Matthew 19:4; Genesis 2:24; and Genesis 2:18. Look for the characteristics of monogamy, permanency, intimacy, and completion.

4. What are some biblical reasons for the institution of marriage? See Genesis 1:27, 28; 1 Corinthians 7:2–5, 9; and the Song of Solomon.

5. If the above questions give us the biblical understanding of what marriage is, then let's look at the possible reasons for the dissolution of that bond. Do the biblical grounds for marriage apply to non-Christians? Laying aside the conventions of our society, what reasons does the non-Christian have for adhering to biblical principles here? Then if two non-Christians do get a divorce, do biblical restrictions concerning divorce apply to them? (This is certainly not meant to encourage non-Christian couples to divorce; it simply points out how illogical it is to hold the non-believers to scriptural behavior patterns when they don't believe in God in the first place.) Think deeply about this before you answer.

6. With the above questions in mind, is a divorce between two non-believers restricted by the Bible? What should our

• • •

response be to those who have experienced divorce before conversion? Read 2 Corinthians 5:17; Ephesians 2:1–7, 19–22; and Psalm 103:10–12. Dwell on what *God's* attitude (not your attitude) is toward those who have sinned—especially in the area of divorce—before they became Christians?

7. Read Matthew 19:3–9. What is the exception for divorce that Jesus states in this passage? Compare this also with Matthew 5:27–32. Note, too, that similar passages (Mark 10:2–12 and Luke 16:18) do not mention adultery's effect on marriage—seemingly allowing this exception to stand.

8. Even though this exception is given in Matthew, does this statement by Christ automatically necessitate divorce when immorality has occurred in a marriage? Remember the verses on forgiveness in the last question. How do these apply to a partner who temporarily strays in his fidelity? What does Jesus say about forgiveness in Matthew 18:21–22? Is forgiveness the better option than divorce when immorality occurs in a marriage? Again, think deeply before answering.

9. Study 1 Corinthians 7:12–15, 39. The overriding emphasis in this passage is obviously to remain in marriage. Even if one mate is not a Christian. However, what is permitted if a non-Christian permanently deserts his mate? Who initiates the action of leaving?

10. In verse 39, the bond of marriage is said to be broken by the death of one partner and there is freedom to remarry. Relate this to the freedom from "bondage" spoken about in 1 Corinthians 7:15 when a desertion occurs.

11. Do Paul's statements in 1 Corinthians 7:12–15 contradict Jesus' words in Matthew 19, seeing that Jesus cited only one exception? Did Jesus' audience differ from that of

● ● ●

Paul's? Was Jesus confronting the situation of a marriage between a believer and a non-believer?

12. Back up to the verses before 1 Corinthians 7:12–15. What is Paul's main thought here? Were the passages about divorce written to provide ways for divorce to occur or were they written to allow for the infections of sin that poison marriage? What is God's ideal for marriage?

13. Is divorce between two Christians who operate on the true basis of love and forgiveness and follow God's will *ever* really an option?

## Thought Questions

14. What if two Christians desire to leave one another because they simply can't get along? Is this grounds for divorce? Are there times when a temporary separation might be necessary? If so, name an example or two.

15. If a Christian desires reconciliation with his partner, but the partner won't respond (even though he or she is a Christian), what options are open to the one desiring reconciliation? Can he or she remarry?

16. Has divorce become "the unpardonable sin"?

17. Does the statement "because of the hardness of your heart" have meaning today?

18. If divorce before conversion is no different than Christian divorce, how do we counsel people who have ruined their marriage already?

19. Is each divorce case to be considered individually?

20. What effect does a divorce have on a person who desires to serve in a church office? Does this situation prevent certain places of service from being open to him/her?

21. How does the teaching of grace apply to divorce? Be

● ● ●

*very* careful here. Be certain that it is grace you are considering and not human license.

22. What other issues grow out of divorce?

## Putting It into Practice

Take a poll of friends and neighbors to determine what the average person on the street thinks about taking the problem of divorce to a church body or group of Christians. Do they sense that they would find acceptance or rejection? Are their expectations of Christian reactions warranted or not? How could these negative attitudes be corrected?

● ● ●

# 10

· · ·

# Commitment Is the Key

## Purposes

To encourage the one characteristic in a marriage union that can make it work—forever.

## Scripture Input

Read Ecclesiastes 5:4, 8:11; Deuteronomy 6:10–15a; Ezekiel 33:30–33; Psalm 56:1–6, 9–11; 1 Corinthians 5:1–7, 6:9–10, 7:3–4, 10–13, 24–35.

1. The message in Ecclesiastes 5:4–5 is very clear: A vow or an oath is a promise that is meant to be kept. Does a marriage vow carry the force of this vow mentioned in Ecclesiastes? Why or why not?

2. Commitment is an old-fashioned word. It is an old-fashioned word that has been watered down by all the public opinion that has washed over it. An erosion has occurred. Moses and the children of Israel faced antagonistic attitudes

· · ·

that were contrary to the plans God had spelled out for them. Read Deuteronomy 6:10–15a. Paul faced a similar problem and wrote 2 Timothy 4:3–4. What did you learn about public opinion in these two sections of Scripture? What is the more trustworthy source for determining your life?

3. Another force that weakens commitment is the tendency to ignore biblical principles and twist doctrinal truth into a more comfortable theology. Ezekiel 33:30–33 depicts a group of people who let their experience block out the truth. Notice verse 31—"(they) hear your words, but they do not do them." What principles of avoiding error-filled theology can be gleaned from the following sections of Scripture? Matthew 15:9; Romans 16:17, 18; 2 Corinthians 2:17, 11:13; Ephesians 4:14; Colossians 2:4, 8; 1 Timothy 6:3, 4; 2 Peter 2:18–19.

4. Commitment can be weakened by our exploitation of God's grace! Because God delays the consequences of sin, many disobey and chuck commitment because they see no immediate bad effects. They accommodate their theology by their experience. Read Ecclesiastes 8:11. Now open your Bible to Psalm 37. Translate the message of the Psalm (the wicked will eventually get their just reward) into your own words. Note especially verses 7–9, 35–36.

5. Lastly, commitment can be weakened by Christian approval of its absence. Paul faced a problem of this scope at the church at Corinth, when a sinful brother had been embraced by fellow Christians and told that "Everything was all right." Hence, 1 Corinthians 5:1–7. What were the consequences for the sinful brother when discipline was finally instituted? What were the consequences for the church outlined by Paul?

• • •

6. On the realistic side, could a spouse's actions ever become so violent (due to emotional sickness or gross demonstrations of sin) that a temporary separation should be considered? Read Psalm 56 and underline the promises given by God for such a crisis time.

7. There are certain realizations which can enhance commitment to your mate. In 1 Corinthians 7:28, 32–35, one discovers a sad, but true, observation about married life: No marriage is conflict-free or distraction-free. But here's the good news. Not one of those conflicts or distractions is insurmountable with Christ. What kind of a picture do the following verses give a Christian about his battles? Matthew 12:20; 1 Corinthians 15:54, 55, 57; 2 Corinthians 2:14; 1 John 5:4.

8. Another realization that aids the commitment factor is that working through a problem, rather than walking out, is God's way of solving any marital difficulty. The general tenor of 1 Corinthians 7:10–13, 24, and 27 is "Hang in there!" It's just like the posters that encourage, "Keep on Truckin!" Take a moment to list the consequences of divorce—the results of walking out—for the husband, the wife, *and* . . . the children. Is it really worth the pain it creates?

9. We have looked at 1 Corinthians 7:3–4 before as a model of unselfishness in marriage. A third realization that cements the commitment bond is to understand that commitment is not a matter of demanding rights . . . but releasing rights. What can we learn from Jesus' attitude of giving up His right to live in Matthew 26:42? How can we apply this attitude of giving up our own rights in marriage? If your marriage is shaky, try hard to be objective and not defensive here.

10. Being committed in marriage glorifies God because it says "God's way is best!" See 1 Corinthians 6:19–20. Think

● ● ●

about how your marriage is or is not an example of the Ephesians 5 analogy. Are you glorifying God? Is that, genuinely, the bottom line goal of your life . . . your marriage . . . your commitment?

## Thought Questions

11. Do a research project on commitment. Have every group member read an avant-garde magazine article about new approaches to marriage. Critique each author's input on how close he adheres to principles that either help or hinder commitment in marriage.

12. Talk with your spouse about making commitment a conscious part of your marriage. What attitudes need renovation or strengthening?

## Putting It into Practice

Write out your commitment to your mate in wording that is similar to wedding vows. Make it as eternal and lasting in tone as you possibly can. Take a quiet time this week to sit down with one another, and declare these vows face to face. Set up a periodic appointment for this practice, perhaps on your birthdays and at your anniversary each year.

> NOTE: Consider having your "vow to commitment" printed nicely and possibly framed. Put it on the dresser in your bedroom or in your wedding album.

• • •

# 11

· · ·

# *Don't Just Get Older, Get Better!*

## Purposes

To take a look at growing older from God's perspective and realize the opportunities out in front for married couples who don't want the pasture after sixty-five!

## Scripture Input

Read Ecclesiastes 11:1–8, 12:1–7.

1. What do the following scriptures teach you about old age and those who are in the later years of life? Exodus 20:12; Leviticus 19:32; Job 12:12; Psalm 71:18, 92:12–14; Proverbs 16:31; 1 Timothy 5:1, 2.

2. Is old age always to be equated with wisdom? Are older people always wiser and more mature in their judgment? In the book of Job, a scene takes place which shows that age does not always mean maturity. A younger man, Elihu, has to counsel his seniors as to their poor "bedside manner"

· · ·

with the ailing Job. This is the setting of Job 32:4–9 (please read). What can an older person learn from this scenario? When is a person "mature"? Relate these insights to fulfillment as an older married couple.

3. After you read Ecclesiastes 12:1–2, put these verses in your own words and on your own level. What is the warning being stated here? What else besides bitterness can make the last years of one's life a sad debacle, so sad that one says "I have no delight in them"?

4. List the physical problems of old age that are being described in Ecclesiastes 12:3–4a, 5b, 6b, 7. Do you get the feeling that a clock is grinding down to a halt? Can you add to this list of physical problems?

5. List the mental and emotional problems being described in Ecclesiastes 12:4b, 5a, and 6a as they relate to old age. Have you been to a rest home lately? Spotted any of these symptoms?

6. Where in the Bible can one find support for any of the many television commercials that spurn getting older and laud all sorts of fountain-of-youth tactics? What happens to those who attempt to dodge the reality of their age and inappropriately attempt to look twenty years younger than they really are? Do they hurt more than just themselves?

7. What can a mate do to help his or her partner face the realities of advancing age?

8. Besides facing reality, another guideline to help you get better as you grow older is to give generously. Read Ecclesiastes 11:1–2 in *The Living Bible* as well as in a standard translation. What does God say about generosity? Take a look at 2 Corinthians 9:7–8 and Hebrews 6:10. What does Luke 12:16–21 say to those of us who are getting older?

9. What else can an older couple give besides money? As

• • •

you read Ecclesiastes 11:1–2, think about the gifts of your time and your experience that can be shared with those younger than you. Now read Romans 12:13 and list some more ways of giving.

10. Ecclesiastes 11:3–4 tells about one who is actually letting life pass him or her by—he has set his mind that the back forty of his life will lie fallow, he will not reap or sow. If you apply 2 Corinthians 9:6 to planning for your future (as well as to giving), what does the Bible say that little planning will yield? What about a *lot* of planning?

11. The picture of Ecclesiastes 11:5–6 is a simple one: The only real security in life is that which is found in trusting God. Compare Proverbs 3:1–2, 9:11, and 10:27 with the Ecclesiastes section. What truths are evident?

12. The final word for getting better as you grow older is to rejoice in that reality—Ecclesiastes 11:7–8. What positives are added to the biblical perspective of rejoicing with the advent of old age when one adds 1 Thessalonians 5:18 to the picture? How is this life view different from Solomon's?

## Thought Questions

13. When do you think you'll be too old to enjoy life? What Scripture will support you at that point and confirm that old age is another *good* part of God's life?

14. Take the 5-fold prescription given for getting better as you get older—live realistically, give generously, adapt willingly, trust fearlessly, rejoice daily. How will this change your attitude toward life today? By the way, take a long look at your face in a mirror. Is there a permanent crease in your forehead? Has a frown replaced that smile on your face? If so ask yourself *why*. Ask God to lighten your life with a renewed zest for living.

• • •

## Putting It into Practice

Arm yourself with this prescription for getting better with increased age, and select someone in your extended family to share the message with this week. Plan a field trip for your discussion group to a rest home—help someone's perspective on life as an older person to grow and get better.

● ● ●

# 12

• • •

*What to Do With an Empty Nest*

**Purposes**

To take one more look at marriage in later years and summarize our findings about marriage for the Christian.

**Scripture Input**

Read Proverbs 24:3–4; James 1:5, 3:17.

1. Look at the stages of marriage suggested in Chapter 12. Where are you? Which stage do you fear the most? Why?

2. What is an "empty nest"? How can a group of couples in this stage of life band together to support one another?

3. The first empty-nest adjustment is said to be decreasing physical attractiveness. For the perceptive Christian woman (and man), how does Proverbs 31:30 apply to this situation?

4. Selfishness is a second hazard of the empty nest. Check the following scriptures and see how they apply to this problem: Romans 12:10, 15:1–3; 1 Corinthians 10:24, 13:4–5; Philippians 2:3, 4.

• • •

5. Boredom, depression, and loneliness are three some-what related problems of the empty nest. Stop and brain-storm right now about ways these dead-end avenues can be avoided as you get older. Are the solutions really tied to retirement monies or to retirement attitudes?

6. Divorce is seen as another adjustment that can droop the sails of any empty-nested couple. Does the presence of children in your home right now add to the cohesiveness of your marriage? What kind of glue would your marriage have if the children were suddenly gone?

7. Meditate on Proverbs 24:3–4 once again. Formulate your own definition of wisdom. How does it square with James's definition (1:5, 3:17)? How can it be employed to help avoid empty-nest struggles in your marriage? Get specific.

8. Refer back to the studies in Chapters 1 and 2 on exer-cising wisdom, employing understanding, and applying knowledge. How can each of these different guidelines help construct a solid foundation for your marriage?

## Thought Questions

9. What new thoughts do you have about God's divine blueprint for marriage that have been gleaned from this study? In what areas is your marriage stronger? In what areas is it still weak?

## Putting It into Practice

Make plans right now for a committed prayer group com-posed of friends you have made in your discussion group. Commit yourselves to a once-a-month gathering for support, strength, and encouragement of strong, healthy marriages.

• • •

# Scripture Index

**Genesis**

1:12 ..............................20
1:18 ..............................20
1:21 ..............................20
1:27–31 ...................87–88
1:31 ..............................20
2 ..................26, 159, 172
2:18–25 ........................19
2:18 ........................20, 21
2:21–22 ........................22
2:24–25 ........24, 29, 35, 86
2:25 ..............................41
3 ................................163
3:9–10 ...........................42
5:1–2 ...........................162
5:3 ..............................162
27 ................................70

**Deuteronomy**

6:10–15 .......................181
24:1–4 ..........................163

**Psalms**

56:1–6, 9–11 .........187–88
103:10–12 ...................167
127:1 .............................30

**Proverbs**

2:6 ................................30
5:1–5 .............................90
11:1 .............................138
14:23 ...................139, 154
15:27 ...........................139
18:14 ...........................124
18:19 ......................124–25
22:7 ....................139, 150
23:4–5 .........................139
24:3–4 ...............26, 34, 48
                        221–22
27:23–24 ......................139
31 ................................58
31:10 .............................57
31:25 .............................57

## Ecclesiastes

5:4 .................................179
5:10 ...............................139
8:11 ...............................184
11 ...............199, 200, 208
11:1–2 ..........................208
11:3 ...............................210
11:4 ...............................210
11:5 ...............................212
11:6 .........................212–13
11:7 ...............................215
12...................199, 200, 206
12:1 ...............................201
12:2 ...............................201
12:3 ...............................202
12:7 ...............................205

## Song of Solomon

2:14 ...............................104
2:15 ...............................104
5:10–15 ...........................91
7:1–9 ...............................92

## Ezekiel

33:30–33 ......................182

## Matthew

19:3 ...............................169
19:4–5 .............................35
19:7 ...............................169
19:8 ...............................162
19:9 .......................168, 175
22:15–22 .............140, 151
22:15–19 ......................151
22:21 .............................152
26:28–29 ......................166

## Luke

19:11–26 ...............142–49

19:11–12 ......................142
19:13 .............................143
19:14 .............................144
19:15 .............................145
19:16 .............................145
19:17 .............................146
19:18 .............................146
19:20–22 ......................147
19:23 .............................148
19:24–25 ......................149
19:26 .............................149

## John

13:34 .............................166

## Acts

10 ...................................89

## Romans

13:6–8 ...................140, 153

## 1 Corinthians

5:1–7 .............................186
6:19–20 ........................194
7:1–2 ...............................93
7:2–3 ...............................95
7:3–4 .......................39, 193
7:4 ...................................95
7:5 ...................................96
7:7 .................................188
7:10–13 ........................191
7:12–15 ........................171
7:15 .......................172, 175
7:24 .............................191
7:26 .............................188
7:27 .............................191
7:28 .............................188
7:32–35 ........................189
7:39 .............................172

● ● ●

**2 Corinthians**

5:17 ......................165, 175
9:6–8 ......................140–41

**Ephesians**

2:1–7 ......................166–67
2:15 ............................166
2:19–22 ........................167
4:24 ............................166
4:25–32 ...................121–22
4:25 ......................122, 123
4:26–27 ........................126
4:26 ............................123
4:28 ............................127
4:29 ............................128
4:30 ............................130
4:31 ............................130
4:32 ............................132
5 ..............................49
5:15–21 ........................105
5:15–16 ........................107
5:17 ............................110
5:18–21 ........................113
5:21 ............................113
5:22–33 ............35, 49, 113
5:22–23 ........................35

**Colossians**

1:18 ............................153

**1 Timothy**

3:4–5 ......................61, 77

**5:8** ..............................75
6:8–10 ..........................141
6:8 ............................156
6:9–10 ..........................156
6:17–19 ........................141
6:19 ............................156

**Hebrews**

13:4 .............................89

**James**

1:5..............................223
3:17 ............................223

**1 Peter**

1:7 ..............................57
1:19 .............................57
3 ..............................49
3:1–9 ......................53, 68
3:1–7 ............................64
3:1–2 ............................69
3:3, 4 ......................56, 70
3:5–6 ............................72
3:6 ............................60
3:7 ..............75, 76, 77, 79
3:8 ............................80
3:9..............................80

**Revelation**

2:17 ............................166
21:1 ............................166

● ● ●

# *Subject Index*

Acceptance, 39
Adam, 20, 21, 23, 24, 26, 30, 39, 41, 42
Admission
  of a problem, 46
Adoration
  as basic role of husband, 50
Adornment, 70
Affair, romantic
  attachment, 42
Affection, 95
Aloneness
  Adam's, 18–22
"American Family, The"
  statistics on divorce, 48
Anger, 123–24
Appearance
  importance of, 55–56, 70
  of the physical body, 91–92
  wife's to husband, 55–56
Arguments, 130–31
Attitude, 56–58

Attractiveness, physical, 218
Beauty, 57
Behavior, 54–55
"Billy Boy," 36
Blueprint, 23, 48, 159, 161
Boredom, 219
Borrowing, 153–54
Bound
  biblical use of, 172
Bride, 22
Business, 144–46
Busyness
  as a termite to marriage, 107–9
Challenge, 13
Christian, 30
Cleave
  biblical use of, 172
  definition of, 37
Commitment, 178–80, 187, 188, 191
  as a bond, 37

● ● ●

illustration of, 37
key to marriage, 159–76
principles of, 188
Communication, 63, 207
Compassionate, 132
Condemnation, 128
Conflict(s)
   marital, 25, 163, 188
Confusion,105–7
Consequences, 184
Creation
   God's approval of, 20
Creature, new, 168
Creditor(s), 153
Criticism, 127

Debts, 153
Depression, 201, 219
Desertion, 171–75
Deterioration
   sexual, 87–97
Devotion, 189
Difference
   between wife and husband,
      23
Divorce, 21, 35, 160, 220–21
   alternatives to, 192
   biblical grounds for, 164–75
   certificate of, 163
   reasons for, 180–86
   statistics on, 48
   when permissible, 164–75
Dress. See appearance.

Essentials
   for life, 27
Eve, 24, 39, 41
Extermination
   of obstacles to marriages,
      114–15

Fashioned
   meaning of, 23
Fellow-heir, 63
Feminists, 22
Fights, in marriage
   methods of attack, 119
   rules for, 121–32
Finances, 135–51
   mismanagement of, 137–38
   planning of, 151–57
   Scriptural principles of,
      151–57
   teaching children
      concerning, 150
Flesh, 39
Fool, 110
Forgiveness, 132
Freedom, 41, 51
Fulfillment, 51

Giving, 208–10
Gloom
   in old age, 201
Glorify, 194–95
Goal(s)
   of wife, 73
   in life, 194–95
Grace, gracious, 132
Growing old, 198
   guidelines for, 208–16
Growing up, 199–200
Guilt, 72, 94, 161, 181, 183

Harmony, 163
Helper,
   definition of, 22
Home
   building house into, 48
   building materials for,
      49–65
   built by wisdom, 26

• • •

council of Solomon, 26
   established by, 26
   filled by, 26
   man's place in, 60
Homosexual, 170
Honesty
   in marriage, 122–23
Honeymoon
   intimacy of, 85
   new name for, 85
   second beginning, 97–100
Honor
   of wife, 63–65, 79–80
Hope, 159
Husband(s)
   basic role of, 50
   building bricks for, 60–64
   not "daddy," 37
   not provider only, 75–76

Image
   of God, 162
Immaturity
   in marriage, 107
   in behavior, 199
Immoral, immorality, 94, 168
Impotence, 205
Intermarriage, Jew and
      Gentile, 163
Inner person
   attractiveness of, 70
Insensitivity
   definition of, 110
   in marriage, 110–14
Intimacy, in marriage. See sex
   biblical principles of, 87–97
   guidelines for, 25, 41–46
   plan of, 97–100
   to be uninterrupted, 96–97
Intimidation, 77–79

Investments, 144, 148–49
Israel, 163

Jealousy, 79–80

Kindness, 133
Knowledge, 25, 28, 48,
      225–26
   husband's of wife, 63

Leadership, 61–62, 77, 78
Likeness, 162
Live, dwell, 60, 76
Loneliness, 219–20
Lord
   as source of skills, 30
   inventor of marriage, 30
Love, 95–96
Lover, 33

Man, 162
Manage, 62
Management, 77
Manipulation
   illustration of, 69
   of husband, 69–70
Marriage
   as a vow, 178–80
   bed, 88, 89
   contemporary concept, 34,
      106–7
   disruption of, 80
   fights in, 118–34
   God's blueprint for, 19
   harmonious, 83
   harmony as meaningful,
      41–43
   intimacy in, 41–46
   ingredients for, 28–29
   inventor of, 30
   myth of, 83

● ● ●

open and broken, 45–46
other than expected, 85
prior to salvation, 165–68
stages in, 217–18
that which strengthens, 103
that which weakens, 104
the person to be changed in,
    30–31
Marital harmony
as meaningful intimacy, 44
described, 40, 41
Marriage contract, vow, 186
statements from, 40
vows of, 102
Maturity, 209
Minister, 62
Money, 136
borrowing of, 153–54
displeasing God without
    management of,
    147–48
God's blessing of
    management of, 149
love of, 156
pleasing God with
    management of,
    146–47
stewards of, 138, 143
teaching children
    management of, 150
wrong attitudes towards,
    141–42
Moses, 24–25
"Musts"
for marriage, 24–25

Naked definition of, 41, 86
Narcissitic woman, 71
Needs
of another, 59
of man, 23

Old Age. See also
growing old, 202–5
"Original match," 160, 162,
    163

Partnership, 61, 78
Permanence
foundational guideline for
    marriage, 25, 37–38
Promiscuity, 93, 94

Rejoice, 215
Relationship
between bride and groom,
    35
in marriage, 19
interpersonal, 106
parent-child, 219
Remarriage, 161, 164–76
Respect
for Christ, 113
mutual, 23
Response
wife toward husband,
    58–60
Retirement, 220
Rights, 193
Romantic, 37, 104

Sacred, 143–44
Sarcasm, 131
Savings, 154–55
Scheming
as a substitute for
    marriage guidelines, 69–70
Secular, 143–44
Self-consciousness, 86
origin of, 41, 42
Selfishness, 80, 193
Self-pity, 223
Severance, 25, 35–37

● ● ●

Sex. See also intimacy
  a view of, 89
  extramarital, 42, 43–44, 93
  marital, 89–92
  premarital, 93–94
Sexual perversion,
  in marriage, 187
Sharing, 76
Sin
  absence of, 42
  consequences of, 164
  effect on marriage, 162–64
  living in, 184–85
Solomon, 26
Spirit
  broken, 124
  gentle, 57, 58, 74
  quiet, 57, 58, 69, 74
Standard, 106
Stubbornness, in marriage,
  113–14
Subjection, 187
Submission
  as basic role in marriage, 49
  missapplication of, 24
Substitutes
  cheap ones, 74, 75, 81–82
  phony ones, 81
  used by husbands, 74–80
  used by wives, 68–74
Surrender, 132, 134
  of rights, 83, 193
  to God, 114

Tact, tactfulness,
  128–30
Taxes, 152–53
Tenderness, 132
Tithes, 152–53
Transparency, 42
Troth
  meaning of, 103
Trust, 112, 129
Truth, 122
Understanding, 26, 28, 48,
  223–25
Uniformity, 39
Unity
  foundational guideline for
    marriage, 25, 38–41
Unrepentant, 168
Unselfishness, 40, 83
Unwholesome, 128
Wedding
  best gift for, 35
  candidates for, 123
Wife
  basic role in marriage of,
    49–50
  behavior toward husband
    of, 54–55
  building bricks for, 54–60
  not as "momma," 37
Wisdom, 26, 28, 48, 122–23
Workaholic, see also busyness,
  110, 220

● ● ●